SOFT SKILLS IN HARD PLACES

THE PERRYVILLE BATTLEFIELD LEADERSHIP EXPERIENCE

COLONEL FRED JOHNSON
UNITED STATES ARMY, RETIRED

Soft Skills in Hard Places

The Perryville Battlefield Leadership Experience

Copyright 2018 by Fred Johnson

Published by Pro Patria Publishing

Editing by:
Mark Ray

First edition, March 2018

ISBN: 978-0-692-07067-3

Created in the United States of America

DEDICATION

For Laura and Madelyn, the eternal source of my softness.

ACKNOWLEDGEMENTS

Perryville is considered one of the best-preserved battlefields in the country. It near-perfectly replicates the physical condition of the site as it was 156 years ago. It is also an exquisitely maintained park that offers magnificent views of the rolling hills of Kentucky's Bluegrass Region. The Perryville Battlefield is a truly wonderful place to visit, if not for its historic value, then for the natural beauty it offers.

The men and women who care for the historic site do not get near the recognition they deserve for their tireless work and passion for history and the preservation of this national treasure. Joan House, Phil Cain, Belinda Warden, Chad Greene, Joe Crafa, Fred Edwards and Faye Hankla are owed immense gratitude for their service to the Commonwealth of Kentucky and the thousands of people from across the country that visit the Perryville Battlefield each year. I am personally grateful to them for their kindness and patience with me as they assisted in my exploration of the landscape and it's historical significance.

I knew almost nothing about the Battle of Perryville when I first visited the park. However, I had the good fortune to meet Chuck Lott, who is a tour guide and the treasurer of the Friends of Perryville, an organization that raises money to maintain the site. Chuck not only looks like a Civil War soldier, he also has an infinite grasp of nearly every detail of the events that took place on those hollowed grounds in October of 1862.

Then, I was reunited with Doug Lippman who also volunteers as a tour guide at the battlefield and is a Civil War re-enactor. Doug taught history at my high school in Centralia, Illinois when I was a teenager. Once I got beyond calling him Doug instead of Mr. Lippman, he joined forces with Chuck and gave me a PhD-level understanding of the battle.

Both men are veterans and our nation owes them a debt of gratitude for their service. However, I am personally thankful for their help, but more so for the enduring friendship that has evolved since we began the project.

Through an email introduction from a friend, Greg Coker and I met at a McDonalds in Harrodsburg, Kentucky. I needed someone to serve as a business subject matter expert for The Perryville Battle Leadership Experience. Greg had all the credentials to fill that role, not to mention he is a dynamic and inspirational speaker. We hit it right off and started putting together the concept for the workshop on napkins over coffee. Then, during the next several months, the idea flourished into what we humbly believe is the best executive leadership seminar in the State. I am blessed to have Greg as a teammate and friend.

The idea for this book came from my association with General

David H. Petraeus (USA, Retired) who demonstrated soft skills in the hardest and most challenging places during his 37 year military career.

Finally, I want to thank Mark Ray for his counsel and hard work as the editor of this book. *Soft Skills in Hard Places* is much better than when I first gave it to him. I am also in debt to Debbie Sawyer, a fellow warrior who had my back and got me out of a tough spot during the preparation of this work.

TABLE OF CONTENTS

FOREWORD

In my book, *The Soft Skills Field Manual*, I talk about *Be, Know, Do*, which is an Army leadership principle I learned from General Richard Cavazos. Cavazos was the Army's first Hispanic Four Star General and a recipient of two Distinguished Crosses (the second highest award for gallantry) along with a Purple Heart and numerous other medals for valor. Clearly, General Cavazos is an expert on leadership and I listened closely to what he had to say.

I have never served in the military. However, I do have over 25 years experience as a senior level executive with three different Fortune 500 Companies and I've led the training and development for over 80,000 employees. I thought I knew all I needed to know about leadership —until I spoke with General Cavazos.

Be, Know, Do is a very simple, but an incredibly powerful way of thinking about leadership.

Be is all about character and the cornerstone to being an effective leader. It is being value based and allows someone to have the courage to do the hard, but right thing under the most difficult circumstances. *Know* is the technical (hard) and interpersonal (soft) skills a leader must possess to be successful. *Do* brings everything together into positive action and enables the person in charge to implement the key components of leadership, providing purpose, direction and motivation for their employees or service members.

Not long ago I met Colonel Fred Johnson, a retired Army officer, with four combat deployments and a whole lot of understanding and practical application of *Be, Know, Do*. Fred proposed that he and I combine our knowledge and experience to form a partnership where we teach leadership and soft skills to business executives and staffs at the Perryville Battlefield Historic Site in the Bluegrass Region of Kentucky.

We called it The Perryville Battlefield Leadership Experience.

The idea was to take a group of corporate leaders on an interactive tour of the Perryville Battlefield and bring them back to a seminar setting to discuss what they learned and how the lessons could be applied to the workplace. Fred would lead the military and historic part of the workshop while I would facilitate the business side of it. However, the real learning would take place in the participant's dialogue about the experience.

Over the next several months Fred and I spent a lot of time together developing the program. It was rewarding seeing the project take shape, but the true gift was the hours spent with Fred hearing his stories and getting to know him. It was truly a blessing. He is a thoughtful person who is passionate about teaching and passing on the lessons of his experience to others and then, in turn, learning from them. Our first client was a company with a nation-wide footprint and a cadre of experienced business leaders. 20 executives from around the country assembled at the Perryville Battlefield on a cool October morning. Fred and I had those healthy pre-game jitters about the endeavor we were about to embark. We had rehearsed, but not before a live audience. With all humility all I can say is —we knocked it out of the ballpark.

The President and CEO of the company, was effusive in his praise. In a review of the event he said:

"The Perryville Battlefield Leadership Experience exceeded all expectations delivering one of the best professional development and leadership workshops we've experienced at Donan Forensic Engineering. Colonel Johnson and Greg Coker are dynamic and inspirational speakers who captivated members of my staff of senior executives from the very beginning of the program. Moreover, the content delivered was well researched to the needs of my company, providing an added value that far exceeded the amount provided in the contract. We cannot wait to use their services again!"

Fred's book, *Soft Skills in Hard Places*, provides the learning framework for The Perryville Battlefield Leadership Experience that we use in our workshops. He makes the Civil War vignettes easily understood by even those who hated history in high school and college. Indeed, this book inspires a love for history and especially its application to present day challenges and a better understanding of leadership. Personally, I can't get enough of it and we are looking to expand our seminars to other historic sites in Kentucky.

Fred incorporates humor and piercing insight to relevant current events with his personal anecdotes that demonstrate the timeless importance of soft skills in leadership. Fred's book is incredibly important and valuable even if you don't plan on participating in the seminar. It certainly will not gather dust on your bookshelf. The lessons it provides are enduring and you will want to revisit them anytime there's an opportunity to impart leadership wisdom to employees or fellow workers.

Soft Skills in Hard Places will help you become a *Be, Know, Do* leader who will build teams that can overcome all obstacles, take any hill, and win every battle in business and the boardroom.

Greg Coker
February 2018

Author of *Building Cathedrals: The Power of Purpose* and the *Soft Skills Field Manual*

www.softskillshq.com

Introduction

Be Hard, Not Stupid

Fresh out of Ranger School as a young lieutenant, I did a training exercise at Fort Drum, New York. It was raining, it was cold and I chose not to put on my wet weather gear. I'd just completed the U.S. Army's most physically difficult leadership course, and I wanted to show my soldiers that I was a tough infantryman. I was, as we called it, being *hard* and embracing the suck.

Struggling to control my shivering through sheer force of will, I sat down with my back against a tree. I pulled out my laminated map to appear as if I was checking our location, but really I was just trying to take my mind off the misery.

Just then, my platoon sergeant, Carlin Brumback, approached me. Brumback was a legend in our organization. It was 1987, just a few years after he had earned a Bronze Star for Valor in a firefight during the invasion of Grenada. He had a reputation for being a rugged warrior who did not know the word fear and could endure insurmountable discomfort. He was the embodiment of *hard*.

He was also fully dressed in a green rain suit on that wet, rainy day at Fort Drum. As I leaned against the tree, the 6' 4", 220-pound Virginian squatted next to me, his elbows resting on his knees. For a long time, he just stared at me. Then, after an uncomfortable and prolonged silence, he reached into my rucksack, which had become soaked in the downpour. He pulled out my wet weather gear and poncho and handed them to me. Then he stood and said, "Sir, being hard doesn't mean you have to be stupid."

Brumback was not being disrespectful or insubordinate. Instead he was giving me the infantry version of tough love. He understood my personal motivation of wanting to be a strong leader. He knew the exact right words to inspire me to put on my wet weather gear and stop looking like an idiot.

Over the next year that I served with Brumback I noticed an incongruity between his exterior appearance of physical strength and how he interacted with his soldiers, coworkers and bosses. His deep southern drawl and extensive use of the military lexicon sometimes disguised his superior intelligence. However, he possessed another kind of intellect that I could not pinpoint but it clearly contributed to his success as a leader.

I never saw Brumback stressed, even in the most trying and chaotic situations. His voice (as deep as it was) was always even, his tone always calm. And he passed that strange serenity to everyone around him. He had a knack of understanding how his small role fit into the larger strategic framework of our organization. He could then articulate our strategy to the most junior person in the workforce and inspire them to achieve tremendous results. He employed his authentic, often-gruff personality to connect with his most senior supervisors. They listened to him and took his advice, and they felt safe that what he said was absolute truth. Brumback was one of the most skilled infantryman I had ever met, well versed in the school-taught tactics of combat. However, he often came up with courses of action that were quite unconventional and they always seemed to work.

Brumback was subordinate to me in rank but, as a warrior, he was superior in every other aspect of our craft. Non-commissioned officers most often shoulder the burden of training their officers. That was the case with Brumback and me. At the time, I didn't really understand the gift he possessed, but I knew that I wanted it. That was the start of my journey to become soft.

"Never trust spiritual leader who cannot dance." — Mr Miyagi

CHAPTER 1

Getting Soft

Back in the mid- to late-80s we said of people like Brumback that they led with their gut. Today, it's called "out of the box" thinking, emotional intelligence and soft skills.

Throughout my 29-year career, which included two deployments to Iraq and one each to Bosnia and Afghanistan, I often thought about that day in the rain with Carlin Brumback and our yearlong service together. As I rose in rank to the grade of colonel, I observed the same attributes that he possessed in other successful leaders. Many of them were my mentors like General David Petraeus (U.S. Army, Retired), who was the senior military commander in both Iraq and Afghanistan and later served as director of the CIA. Others were career-enlisted personnel like Brumback.

The irony is not lost on me that many warriors who would be called *hard* by virtue of their physical and moral strength can also display a quality that is described as *soft*. In fact, I have learned that these traits are not mutually exclusive; they actually complement each other in a way that produces a remarkable degree of effectiveness.

Hard people can have soft skills, and they demonstrate them in hard places like combat and in the business boardroom.

Soft skills are those personal attributes that enable someone to interact effectively and harmoniously with other people and allow for good decision making and problem solving. They are intangible talents that often manifest in what is called emotional intelligence. They include:

- Creative and innovative thinking
- Problem identification and solution finding
- Communication, both verbal and active listening
- Negotiation
- Initiative
- Risk management
- Relationship building
- Cultural and diversity awareness
- Adaptability
- Flexibility
- Empathy
- Stress management
- Conflict resolution
- Change management
- Recognizing personal and organizational blind spots
- Leadership and followership

Many of the soft skills are associated to one another and if you possess one there is a likelihood that you have the other. For example, negotiation and relationship building are closely linked.

Hard and Soft

In addition to soft skills there are also hard skills (not to be confused with the physical and mental toughness of military *hard*). These are normally technical in nature and learned in school or as a trade apprentice—skills like writing, math, reading, electrical work, plumbing, welding, programming, practicing medicine, legal analysis, etc. They are specific to the job at hand and can be defined and measured

So why are soft skills important if the execution of the hard skill is the primary purpose of a person's employment? The answer is pretty straightforward: we live in a world where our interactions with other people affect workplace harmony and effectiveness.

Stanford Research International made the claim that 75 percent of long-term job success depends upon soft skills mastery, while only 25 percent relies on technical skills.

But why?

There are certainly jobs within unique organizations where employees do their work without ever dealing with other coworkers. Entire careers may be spent in this kind of isolation, but they are rare. And even those workers confined to cubicles will surely have to answer to a boss. They will have to know how to be a follower and communicate effectively. Moreover, those technical specialists may rise in the corporate ladder one day and assume positions of leadership. What then? Do we wait until they are in charge of people to teach how to lead them?

Even in Army basic training aspiring soldiers are at times put in positions of leadership . To be sure, they were first drilled with the discipline to be good followers and understand their place within a team. Regardless, they had to experience what it was like to lead.

This was particularly the case when I was in command during the surge in Iraq and many young men and women went to war not long after graduating from boot camp. It's a grim fact of war that leaders die. The military learned long ago that it is imprudent to wait until soldiers are responsible for the lives of others to teach them how to lead and care for them. The same holds true in any organization. Great leaders train their replacement, but first those in charge must master both hard and soft skills themselves.

In the military, an artillery officer has to know how to fire a cannon, maintain it and repair minor malfunctions. The officer must know how to operate a fire-direction computer and understand where best to position the cannon so its effects are maximized. However, officers must also lead soldiers and coordinate with supported units whose leaders often outrank them. And they have to advise those leaders, who sometimes think they know more than artillerymen, on how to best employ the weapon system. They have to mentor, coach and teach someone who outranks them. These are skills that are not easily taught, but they are as vital to mission success as the technical aspects of operating the weapon system.

Is the need to be proficient in both hard and soft skills any less important in the business boardroom? Or at the factory? Or in restaurants, hotels or hospitals? Obviously not.

So how does one acquire soft skills?

Hard skills are pretty straightforward. You go to school, there's a teacher and curriculum, and you must pass a test or earn a certification. But how does a person learn to be empathetic, communicate verbally as well as non-verbally, or know how to identify blind spots in oneself and their organization? These are things we normally think our parents, siblings, mentors, and often experience teach us. There are certainly those that are born with these abilities, like a child prodigy who can solve difficult physics problems having never taken a formal math class.

But can soft skills be taught through traditional methods like lecture or rote classroom instruction? Can PowerPoint slides create the conditions that enable someone to know the right thing to say at the right moment? Can reading a book about active listening make someone a better active listener?

Common educational practices will surely help people know the meaning behind particular soft skills, but they fall short instilling those attributes into everyday practice. To fundamentally change how one effectively interacts with others or solve complex problems requires a combination of methods.

Recognizing soft skill shortfalls. To fix a problem in oneself, an individual has to recognize there is an issue. It is difficult for someone to realize they have interpersonal and leadership challenges. The 360 assessment I took in the U.S. War College helped me. Employees, peers, and bosses rated me on a variety of leadership traits and then provided written comments on my strengths and weaknesses. The results were far worse than I anticipated; I was not the quality of leader I had thought. Nevertheless, areas of emphasis were identified that required my attention, and I was bound and determined to improve them. There are other assessment tools that are effective. However, the most impactful path to social self-awareness is being told by one's boss that there are challenges that need to be addressed.

The Army requires individuals to be formally counseled in writing by their direct supervisor every three months. Frankly, I did not particularly enjoy participating in those sessions, nor did I like leading them. More often than not, there were far more areas that required improvement than those that merited accolades. It's true that the truth hurts, but it is a surefire way to get a person's attention. Clearly, there is an art to counseling. It is, in fact, a soft skill that many leaders are woefully poor at doing. Nevertheless, it is absolutely required as a key step in improving both hard and soft skills.

Mentoring and modeling. I was blessed to have great mentors who modeled the soft skills necessary for being an effective leader. Most were also great at counseling. However, one of the best and most innovative mentors I ever had was General David H. Petraeus.

In 1991, not long after we returned from Desert Storm, the first Gulf War in Iraq, I assumed command of an infantry company, about 135 people, in the storied 101st Airborne Division (Air Assault). A month or so later Petraeus, then a lieutenant colonel, took command of the battalion, which had 600 soldiers assigned. In our first meeting, I gave Petraeus a briefing on my unit that provided an overview of key personnel, our readiness status, and planned training events. This briefing gave me the chance not only to provide an accurate assessment of a unit's capabilities but also to make an immediate connection with my commander and gain his trust.

During the meeting, I was not sure if I was making the impression I had hoped. Petraeus always seemed to be a slide or two ahead of me in the briefing. He would say "Got it" before I had even gotten through the point I was trying to make. I felt that I was briefing a computer that processed information faster than a human can think. I couldn't keep up with the guy.

When I was done, Petraeus pushed the briefing packet to the side of the table and said, "All great stuff, Fred. Just great." Then he got up and went to his desk. I thought, "Shit, I really blew it."

But he wasn't done. He picked up a book, brought it over, and handed it to me. "Fred, have you ever read Richard Haliburton's *Royal Road to Romance*?" he asked. "No, sir," I replied, wondering why he'd just given me this yellow-paged, dog-eared book that looked like it had come from a garage sale. "Look it over and tell me what you think," he said, followed by "Great meeting, company commander. Well done."

That was it. The briefing was over and I left thinking *what the hell*?

About a week later, my phone rang. It was 6:30 on Saturday morning, and I was getting ready to work out. The voice on the other end said, "Fred, this is LTC Petraeus. Meet me at the battalion headquarters. Let's go for a run. Bring the book. See you in 15 minutes." I could barely say yes before he hung up.

When I arrived at the battalion area, Petraeus was out front doing pushups. He met me as I got out of my car and asked if I knew a good 10-mile run route. When I told him I did, we took off running at a reasonable and conversational pace. I didn't even have time to stretch or warm up.

As we started a long uphill climb, Petraeus asked, "So what did you think of Haliburton's book? What was your major takeaway?"

Now, I should explain the book, which I had fortunately read before our surprise meeting. Richard Haliburton was an adventurer and world explorer in the 1930s. He swam the full length of the Panama Canal, circumnavigated the globe as a co-pilot in a biplane, and died while attempting to sail a Chinese junk across the Pacific Ocean from Hong Kong to San Francisco. *The Royal Road to Romance* was one of many he wrote about his adventures.

In response to Petraeus' question, I said, "I think Haliburton was an adrenalin junkie. He went from one adventure to the next to get his fix. He's a great writer and the stories are awesome, but I'm not sure what he accomplished other than that. It's not like he discovered the cure to cancer or anything."

My answer brought a noticeable increase in Petraeus' pace. I adjusted mine to his, and he asked, "Did you like the book, Fred?" I nodded yes as Petraeus moved the speed to the next higher gear. He then asked *why* I liked it.

I was starting to feel the stress of the run now. We were running at least a six-minute mile pace. I consciously made myself relax as to not outwardly show I was getting my ass kicked. Petraeus' questions became more and more abstract, requiring me to talk more during my answers. Keeping my breathing as even as possible, I tried to be succinct in my responses to conserve my energy, but he would not let me get by without me expanding on my answers.

When we had about a mile left in the run, the questions about the book stopped. In fact, there was no more talking. We were running a sub six-minute pace now, and our run had become a race. I forgot that Petraeus outranked me and was my boss. At a street corner, I purposely cut him off, hugging the inside of the turn and bumping his arm. His sweat mixed with mine. He drooled spit from his mouth like a frothing thoroughbred horse.

At the next turn he gave me an elbow, which threw off my pace. I was close to that point of panic when the pain from near-complete exhaustion produces a copper taste in your mouth. The battalion headquarters was in sight, only a couple hundred yards ahead of us. It was now an all-out sprint. We were side by side at the end, but as we crossed the imaginary finish line, Petraeus leaned forward as if he were breaking the tape at the end of a race.

My battalion commander had just run a much younger person into the ground. There was little question left in my mind that David Petraeus was hard.

But Petraeus was also soft.

I didn't think about it at the time, but there was a whole lot of soft skill counseling, mentoring, and modeling that went on during that hour's worth of running. It was not long before I realized every encounter with Dave Petraeus was a learning opportunity and sometimes even a test. Afterwards he would say, "Okay, now that we're done, let's do an after-action review." In this particular instance, we talked about the run and what I had learned from it.

So what did I learn?

First, Petraeus demonstrated that one must lead by example and that hardship has to be shared. Effective leaders do not ask their men and women to do something they are unwilling to do themselves. This was a great lesson in empathy. Too often leaders ask their people to perform a difficult task without understanding the physical and emotional effects it has on them. Then they wonder why they failed.

Second, Petraeus showed approachability and an openness to reasonable conflict. There are not many leaders who would allow a subordinate to elbow them in the gut. This aspect of his character was displayed throughout his career in other ways. He created an environment where you could speak your mind as long as you did so in a respectful and productive way. "There are no bad ideas here," he would tell us. "You're not going to hurt my feelings. Say what you're thinking."

Third, Petraeus created an artificially stressful environment to have a conversation that required thoughtful reflection. It would have been very different talking about Halliburton swimming across the

Panama Canal over coffee than it was climbing a hill at a six-minute-a-mile pace. It is also challenging giving an order to attack with bullets flying and rockets are exploding around you. During difficult physical training exercises Petraeus would remind us to relax; in doing so he helped us learn to manage stress. In these instances, he took an indirect approach to achieve his coaching and mentoring goals. He would never say, "I'm putting you through all this pain and suffering so you will learn to be calm under fire." He would simply establish the conditions for us to learn the lessons on our own.

Petraeus knew that soft skills were particularly important in hard places where leaders have to manage stress and control emotional response to be an effective. Therefore, he created artificial environments to replicate those conditions.

The Petraeus Process

The way Petraeus taught those soft skill lessons on the run that day was truly remarkable, innovative, and by no means an accident. We learn by doing and through action. He would repeat similar learning scenarios throughout the year I spent under his command and in other assignments I served with him.

First, he had me read a book that had absolutely nothing to do with the military and, on the surface, little to do with leadership.

(Commanders in my previous units had reading lists, but they all pertained to war.) Then, without any warning of his intention and under the duress of running a six-minute-mile pace, he asked me to reflect on the book, its author, and what I had learned about his character. This took me totally by surprise, and I had to think on my feet out of fear that I might disappoint him. During our run and discussions afterward—and it seemed that we always came back to that damn book—we talked about Halliburton's courage, creative thinking, and willingness to take risks. And in turn we spoke about how those traits applied to leading soldiers.

The process took me completely out of my comfort zone and made me think outside the box. And nearly 30 years later I am still talking about Richard Halliburton, the *Royal Road to Romance*, and what the experience taught me. I called it the Petraeus Process, and what I learned through the method he applied was lasting and impactful. However, at the time I didn't know the Petraeus Process was adapted from a time-tested approach to learning.

Experiential Learning

Aristotle wrote in the Nicomachean Ethics, "For the things we have to learn before we can do them, we learn by doing them." This is the foundation of experiential learning theory, which David Kolb posited in 1984. The model describes a four-stage learning cycle:

- Have a concrete experience
- Reflect on the experience
- Develop an abstract conceptualization on the experience
- Actively experiment with your new understanding of the experience

I believe the Petraeus Process is a form of experiential learning.

In the case of the run, the concrete experience was the interaction with my boss where we discussed complex subject matter in an uncomfortable environment that required me to think on my feet (and on the run). Petraeus created conditions similar to the decision-making and problem-solving that are experienced in combat. Reflection and abstract conceptualization occurred near simultaneously to the experience. Examples of Halliburton's personal courage and his search for adventure were compared and contrasted with military leadership traits. The teaching points were reinforced during the after-action review. Active experimentation came later as I applied the lessons to leading my soldiers. The results of the experimentation were further evaluated during my quarterly counseling with Petraeus.

The effectiveness of the Petraeus Process is legendary in the military. Petraeus was called the "General Maker" because so many of his protégés went on to make Flag Officer and serve at the highest levels of our armed forces. I was promoted to colonel, a rank that was most likely far beyond my reach by natural abilities alone. I owe much of my success to have been an alumnus of the Petraeus Process.

The Petraeus Process is best-applied one on one between mentor and mentee. However, a similar approach can be used in larger groups (and there is no requirement to run).

The Staff Ride

The military has long used the staff ride as a training approach to leadership development. It immerses participants into historical combat situations where they are required to look through the eyes of the men and women who fought the battle that is being studied. Events and decisions made by the people in charge are analyzed and dissected by staff ride participants. It is part case study, part lecture, and part interactive roleplaying.

The staff ride starts when the facilitator chooses a battlefield. This can be almost any location where a combat activity took place, provided the site is maintained to approximate its appearance at the time of the battle. Gettysburg, Antietam, and the site of Custer's Last Stand are very popular staff ride locations. However, nearly every state has historic sites commemorating battles dating from the French and Indian Wars through the Civil War, as well as battles with the Native Americans. Honestly, the actual battle is irrelevant;

nearly all encounters where the wills of men and women are tested on the field combat present the opportunity to learn something, especially the soft skills of leadership and problem-solving.

Weeks before the start of the actual staff ride, the members of the organization that will participate in the event are given reading materials about the battle and are assigned specific leaders to study. On the day of the staff ride, the group moves to selected locations on the battlefield. Members then deliver a brief about their designated individual and describe that individual's actions at the point in the battle. Discussions about tactics like the use of terrain, employment of artillery, and infantry maneuver normally follow. There is also dialogue about decision-making and leadership.

However, what makes a staff ride more effective than just reading a case study is that you are actually immersed in the environment where those actions took place. You can see, feel, touch, and sometimes even hear what was going on the day of battle all those years ago.

It is a larger-scale application of the Petraeus Process.

Playing Benedict Arnold

During my Army career I must have gone on at least 20 staff rides. They were a routine part of our annual leadership development training in most units that I served. My first staff ride was with the organization to which Carlin Brumback and I were assigned. During the summer of 1988 we traveled to the Revolutionary War battlefield of Saratoga in upstate New York.

I was assigned the role of Benedict Arnold, who was a brigadier general in the Continental Army. Frankly, at the time, all I knew about Arnold was that he is considered one of the greatest traitors in American history. However, part of the staff ride methodology is that you learn as much as possible about the leader you are assigned to portray and become intimately familiar with their actions during the battle. While Arnold might have become a turncoat later in his career, his leadership was the deciding factor in the Americans' decisive victory over the British in both the First and Second Battles of Saratoga on September 19 and October 7, 1777.

Interestingly, it was not Arnold's tactical decision-making and leadership that yielded the greatest insights. Rather, it was his interaction with his boss, General Horatio Gates, where the most important and lasting learning points were made.

At the start of the First Battle of Saratoga, the British attacked the Americans with a superior force. General Gates wanted to be patient and wait, but Arnold, who was second in charge, disagreed and wanted to attack. A shouting match followed, and after several hours of arguing Arnold finally convinced his boss to adopt a more aggressive course of action. The result was that 550 British soldiers were killed compared to 280 lost by the Americans.

Even though Arnold's actions yielded a positive result, Gates relieved him of command because of the disagreement and disrespect shown by his subordinate. Tension remained high between the two until the start of the second battle. Arnold was eager to get in the fight, so he swallowed his pride and asked Gates if he could go forward and observe the action. Gates was reluctant but allowed him to go. While Arnold was only supposed to watch, he got involved in the fray and, even though he was severely wounded, his bravery and leadership contributed to a strategically significant American victory.

Gates never gave credit to Arnold, the Army and Congress never recognized Arnold's contributions at Saratoga, and he was passed over for command. Arnold felt slighted. In 1780 he tried to hand over the American-held fort of West Point to the British. After his plot failed, he became known as the most famous traitor in American history. He later died destitute in London in 1801.

As we stood near the location of where Arnold led the counterattack, I discussed how he positioned his forces and led a charge only to be stopped by fortified obstacles. Seeing an opening and exploiting it as bullets rained against his forces, he gained surprise and rolled up the British flank. I then explained aspects of basic infantry tactics that were used.

I thought my presentation was effective, but I stumbled when my boss inquired if there was anything else I learned other than tactics.

Thankfully, Carlin Brumback was by my side and blurted out, "You don't piss off your commander, even when you're right. Ole Benedict Arnold wouldn't be remembered as a cowardly turncoat if he'd thought a bit before he opened his trap."

Brumback's remark produced hilarious laughter (as he always did). When everyone had settled down, our commander, a lieutenant colonel at the time who had several tours in Vietnam and later achieved the rank of major general, then spoke. Building on Brumback's comment he told us, "Disagreement doesn't mean disrespect. Even though Arnold's tactical instincts were on the money, he didn't have the personal discipline or ability to explain them to Gates in a convincing way. Benedict Arnold's failing was that he couldn't help his boss to see what he was seeing."

Our commander continued and talked about how Arnold's leaders failed him, as well. "Gates ruined the career of a great soldier because he couldn't get passed the incident," he said. "He couldn't put it behind him. So, instead of pulling Arnold up after he fell, Gates just pushed him down further. I wonder what history would say about Benedict Arnold if his superiors were a little more kind and provided more leadership in handling the situation."

In that brief interaction, several soft skills were identified and addressed:

- Communication, both verbal and active listening

- Negotiation
- Relationship building
- Conflict resolution
- Leadership and followership

The final, and most important, phase of a staff ride is to discuss the lessons learned and how they apply to organizational effectiveness. Each participant would have to write an after-action review and the key points would be addressed in following professional development classes and counseling throughout the year.

I titled my after action review *Playing Benedict Arnold*. In a rare intellectual and reflective moment at that time (I was 25, an infantryman and a first lieutenant after all—not too far separated from my college partying days), I wrote that being an effective leader is often like performing a role in a play.

For example, in Shakespeare's *Julius Caesar*, Marc Antony famously turns the crowd against Brutus and his group of conspirators in his *Friends, Romans, and Countrymen* speech. Antony does this without ever personally attacking Brutus. In fact, he compliments his enemy repeatedly, "Brutus is an honorable man." In the end, the crowd comes to support Antony and his cause.

Antony showed great restraint controlling his anger. After all, Brutus and his crew killed Julius Caesar, Antony's mentor and dear friend. He understood the audience he was addressing. The crowd supported

Brutus during his remarks earlier and insulting him could enrage the crowd. Rather, he played on their sympathy. He connected with them on an emotional, but positive, level. Finally, he employed superior verbal communication skills that were inspiring. Ultimately, the crowd changed their minds and backed Antony.

I concluded my paper, asserting effective leaders must be capable of playing various roles in their interactions with their soldiers—one part does not accommodate all situations. And the art of leadership is knowing which role to play and when.

The Saratoga staff ride had a profound effect on my understanding of leadership. I had previously thought leading infantrymen was just about being a great marksman, knowing how to navigate and calling for artillery support. However, I learned that becoming a truly great leader requires much more than technical and tactical competence.

When I retired from the Army in 2014, I went to the Perryville Battlefield and toured it with a friend who was a very successful businessman in Louisville. He commented, "There's a lot to learn here and more than just about the Civil War." The idea struck me then that the historic site would be a perfect place to bring the Petraeus Process and the staff ride experience to teach leadership to corporate executives and their staffs.

CHAPTER 2

The Perryville Battlefield Leadership Experience

The Perryville Battlefield Leadership Experience provides a framework for leaders of industry and business to incorporate the principles of the Petraeus Process and the staff-ride methodology in teaching soft skills to the men and women within their organizations. Specifically, the 1862 Civil War battle that took place in Perryville, Kentucky is the focus of study, and the historic battlefield site is used as the classroom for instruction. Other examples from history and my personal experience during my 29-year Army career and multiple combat tours are also incorporated in the event. The intent is to further bolster the relevance of current-day military events with the Civil War battle and show that the importance soft skills is timeless.

The Perryville Battlefield Leadership Experience is also for veterans transitioning out of the armed forces to the civilian workplace. After retiring from the Army, I made the conscience decision not to seek employment with the military as a government service civilian or contractor, which is a natural path for many retirees. It's usually a seamless transition. However, I wanted to see if my skills as a soldier transferred to the private sector. It was truly an experiment I wanted to try. To that end, I found my military experience to be an asset in some areas and a liability in others.

My Army service taught me how to lead and leverage many soft skills, such as oral and written communication, empathy, and problem identification and solving. I spent over four years during my 29-year career in Army professional development schools. Compared to civilian companies, that is a remarkable investment for an organization to make in an employee. I earned two master's degrees, and the Army paid for both of them.

Nonetheless, I struggled in critical soft skills that caused me challenges in the civilian workplace. Overconfidence in my abilities was the most problematic, and the consequences of hubris contributed to poor followership, weak conflict resolution, especially with fellow coworkers, and inadequate emotional response control. Overall, I did not clearly see myself and the adverse effect I sometimes had on the mission.

One of the reasons I wrote this book was to better understand how soft skills are developed in people. I wanted to know if there was something I could have done differently to prepare myself for the transition from the military. Moreover, I wanted to pass that knowledge on to civilian executives and the veterans who will work for them.

The Battle of Perryville was fought on October 8, 1862 in the Bluegrass Region of the state between the Army of the Ohio, led by

Don Carlos Buell, and the Army of the Mississippi, led by Braxton Bragg. The conflict was bloody and costly for both sides. In the end, the South scored a tactical victory, but it endured a lasting strategic loss to the Union forces. The battle is considered the high water mark of the Confederacy in the West.

The Confederates left Kentucky, never to return.

Using combat events that took place over 150 years ago, participants in the Perryville Battlefield Leadership Experience are immersed in an innovative and unique experiential learning environment. During the program, they walk in the steps of leaders of the Confederate and Union armies as they fought this strategically important encounter. Then they analyze those leaders' decisions and compare and contrast them with their own personal approaches to decision-making and leadership. The end result is an executive, or aspiring executive, who is better prepared to lead in the 21st century.

There is no other staff retreat that can provide the outcomes offered by the Perryville Battlefield Executive Leadership Experience. It is a tailorable program designed to address specific corporate professional development needs with overall deliverables that include:

A More Confident Employee Who is Prepared to Lead: This experiential learning opportunity allows participants to acquire executive leadership lessons by being immersed in an environment that requires them to analyze decisions that were made on the battlefield by Civil War leaders. They will provide their perspective to the group and get feedback. The participant will have to look at problems differently and be required to think outside the box.

A Better-Understood Corporate Vision: Corporate leaders engage with their staffs and employees about the organizational mission and vision using relevant Perryville battlefield activities. Participants are able to literally experience the corporate leader's strategic intent by identifying similarities and differences in the plans of the Civil War military personnel in charge.

A Chance to Really Think Outside the Box: Participants will be required to think on their feet during the experience as they discuss the Civil War military leader they were assigned to study. They will also be immersed in a learning environment that may not be comfortable for them, specifically complex military operations.

A Coaching Opportunity: Corporate leaders will be able to observe individuals' reaction to complexity and unfamiliar data. This offers the senior executive a chance to coach their employees in a nonthreatening environment.

A More Cohesive Team: Shared learning in an immersive, non-traditional classroom environment offers an excellent opportunity for team building. Other events, such as marching and musket handling and loading, may be included as a part of the experience.

A Better Appreciation for Kentucky's Rich History: Participants will become better acquainted with Kentucky and its importance in the course of historical events.

To achieve these outcomes, a very detailed methodology has been developed for the Perryville Battlefield Leadership Experience.

Methodology

- The first step in the program is to meet with the senior executive to identify their training objectives for the experience. Seminar mentors and facilitators will become familiar with the corporate culture, vision, and mission prior to the meeting to help the corporate leader tailor the outcomes and deliverables they want to attain. The facilitators will then identify relevant battlefield events that will address the senior executive's desired teaching points

- Participants read *Soft Skills in Hard Places*. They may supplement their understanding of the battle by reviewing Kenneth Noe's *Perryville: This Grand Havoc of War*.

- Participants may be assigned specific leaders to study prior to the event. However, there is some benefit in designating those battlefield personalities to group members of the day of the event.

- On the day of the event, the group will meet at the Perryville Battlefield at 9 a.m. and assemble in a classroom where they are given a brief orientation of the day's activities.
- The group will then be led on a tour of the battlefield to locations of significant combat actions. At each stop the group will provide a brief orientation and description of the events that took place at the site.
- The participants will then return to the classroom.
- The group will participate in a discussion of key executive leadership competencies and best corporate practices.
- The group will break into smaller sections where they will discuss assigned topics (leadership, corporate best practices, company mission and vision) in context of the battlefield tour and overview. The group will then brief their takeaways.
- The senior executive's participation throughout the process is the most important component of the experience. While they will not have a specific role, they will guide the discussion when they deem appropriate to emphasize particular points relevant to their corporate, culture, mission, and vision.

CHAPTER 3
How to Use this Book

Soft Skills in Hard Places is the primer for the Perryville Battlefield Leadership Experience. Although the vignettes are historically accurate, this is not a history book. Instead, the book's intention is to use the combat actions that took place in Perryville, Kentucky on October 8, 1862 to derive soft skill and leadership lessons, nothing more.

The book focuses on only one part the battle, as well. The opening actions and combat activities on the Union's left flank were the most decisive and provided the best examples of leaders using soft skills in the bloodiest and most difficult places of the engagement. There were other instances during the battle of soft skill excellence or failure, but they are not all examined in this work.

Leaders of industry and business can use this book to lead their own staff ride. However, the experience is more effective when facilitated by a team of experts who know the battlefield and the events that took place there and who are skilled at leading workshops. These battlefield experts can help fill any gaps in information that participants may have questions, while keeping the focus on learning lessons in soft skills and leadership.

That said, it is possible to use the book to take a self-guided tour of the battlefield, especially when the book is complemented with other readings or a visit to the Perryville Battlefield Historic Site Museum. Markers are placed throughout the park and a map is available at the museum, and there is a Perryville Battlefield smartphone app that will greatly enable an unassisted excursion. Nevertheless, a solo adventure on the grounds may not provide the experiential learning opportunity that occurs in a group setting led by a skilled escort.

How the Book Is Structured

Soft Skills in Hard Places starts with a very simple chronology of the Civil War up to the Kentucky Campaign. This is done to provide a context, particularly for readers who are unfamiliar with this time in history. Some of the events, like the Emancipation Proclamation, play a role in the discussion of the significance of Perryville.

Next are short personality profiles of the leaders that participated in the events that took place during the battle. These descriptions are very important to the learning process. In most cases, the information provided in the biographies will inform staff-ride participants as to why each man made the decisions he did based on his character. They will help identify whether or not the leader effectively employed soft skills. They will assist with getting into the mind of the person being studied and allow group members to see themselves through the eyes of the combatant.

Then there is a brief overview of events specific to the Western Theater of the Civil War and the invasion of Kentucky. The summary is followed by a series of vignettes of the actions that took place on the battlefield.

These snippets of the activities will be reviewed and discussed at specific locations on the battlefield during the Perryville Battlefield Leadership Experience, and this is where the learning really starts.

Touring the Battlefield

Whether you visit the battlefield alone or as part of the Perryville Battlefield Leadership Experience, it is very important to take in every aspect of the battlefield.

The lay of the ground played an important role in the battle. The first thing to notice is the terrain, particularly the rolling hills and the steepness of some of the climbs. Look at the natural and manmade obstacles. The fence that runs across the battlefield is very important and so is the vegetation with briar patches and tall grass. Soldiers had to assault up these inclines, over the fences, and through the thorny fields.

Consider the weather as well. It was very hot that time of the year in 1862. One of the worst droughts in history had just occurred, and many water sources had largely dried up. Some historians claim the battle actually started over water. In fact, when the soldiers came to Perryville, the water they found was in scarce stagnant pools. Scum had to be scraped of the top and boiled so as not to cause sickness. To exacerbate the situation temperatures for the week preceding the battle were in the 90s. On the day of the battle the temperature would be 85 degrees. Imagine the young men literally dying of thirst when also facing death in the attack.

Think about the distances the soldiers had walked in a very short time. Most of the Union forces came down from Louisville and trudged those 90 miles over the gravel of unpaved roads. Over the course of the summer the iron tires of the wagon traffic had ground the gravel into a choking ankle-deep limestone dust. The Confederates walked 60 miles under the same conditions from Bardstown—and this was after entering Kentucky from Tennessee. . Reflect on how it would feel—sore and blistered feet, tired and hungry—and then being told you must face death.

Perryville is one of the best-preserved historic battlefield sites in America. However, there are some features that no longer remain. For example, there was a cornfield that played an important role in the fight that isn't there anymore. It is important to imagine those aspects of the terrain as being present.

Also consider the equipment the soldiers carried and the wool uniforms they wore. Some had shoes, and others did not. There were men that were well seasoned and trained, and others that had just left home and never fired their weapon. At least one unit was comprised of Germans, many of whom didn't speak English but had fought long and hard during the Revolution of 1848 in Europe.

Finally, try to understand the physical and emotional effects of close combat. Musket fire from hundreds of men fired simultaneously. Cannons let loose exploding shells, canisters that expended dozens of ball-bearing-sized projectiles like a shotgun. Rounds rolled through formations like bowling balls. Contemplate the deafening noise and dense smoke. Envision being surrounded by the dead and dying, stepping over and through mutilated bodies, and watching your friends killed.

It is absolutely imperative that these components of war be considered when reflecting on the vignettes and what they mean. While the business workplace is not as nearly frightening and difficult (one would hope!), it is filled with its own hazards. There is a different kind of fog and friction. For the Perryville Battlefield Leadership Experience to achieve its full effect, the emotional connection with the conditions of combat that took place on October 8, 1862 must be made.

The men who fought at Perryville were certainly hard, but more often than not it was soft skills that got them up the hill. *Soft Skills in Hard Places* is about the human dimension of war and how business leaders can apply the lessons from the Battle of Perryville to their workplace and the professional development of their employees.

CHAPTER 4

The Civil War up to the Battle of Perryville

The Battle of Perryville didn't occur in a vacuum. In order to understand the events of October 8, 1862, you must first understand what had happened over the previous 23 months. Here's a brief synopsis.

November 6, 1860: Abraham Lincoln is elected sixteenth president of the United States. He is the first Republican president in the nation and represents a party that opposes the spread of slavery in the territories of the United States.

December 17, 1860: The first Secession Convention meets in Columbia, South Carolina.

December 20, 1860: South Carolina secedes from the Union.

January 1861: Six additional Southern states secede from the Union.

February 8-9, 1861: The Confederate States of America is formed when the Southern states that seceded create a government at Montgomery, Alabama.

February 18, 1861: Jefferson Davis is appointed the first President of the Confederate States of America, a position he will hold until elections can be arranged.

March 4, 1861: Abraham Lincoln is inaugurated as the sixteenth president of the United States in Washington, D.C.

April 12, 1861: Southern forces fire upon Fort Sumter, South Carolina. The Civil War formally begins.

April 15, 1861: President Lincoln issues a public declaration that an insurrection exists and calls for 75,000 militia to stop the rebellion. As a result of this call for volunteers, four additional Southern states secede from the Union in the following weeks. Lincoln will respond on May 3 with an additional call for 43,000+ volunteers to serve for three years, expanding the size of the regular Army.

May 24, 1861: Union forces cross the Potomac River and occupy Arlington Heights, the home of future Confederate General Robert E. Lee. It is during the occupation of nearby Alexandria that Colonel Elmer Ellsworth, commander of the 11th New York Infantry and a close friend of the Lincolns, is shot dead by the owner of the Marshall House just after removing a Confederate flag from its roof.

June 3, 1861: A skirmish near Philippi in western Virginia is the first clash of Union and Confederate forces in the east.

June 10, 1861: **Battle of Big Bethel**, the first land battle of the war in Virginia.

June 20, 1861: At the culmination of the Wheeling Convention, the region that composes the northwestern counties of Virginia breaks away from that state to form West Virginia. It will be officially accepted as the thirty-fifth state of the Union on June 20, 1863.

July 21, 1861: **Battle of Bull Run (or First Manassas)** is fought near Manassas, Virginia. The Union Army under General Irwin McDowell initially succeeds in driving back Confederate forces under General Pierre Gustav Toutant Beauregard, but the arrival of troops under General Joseph E. Johnston initiates a series of reverses that sends McDowell's army in a panicked retreat to the defenses of Washington. It is here that Thomas Jonathan Jackson, a professor at Virginia Military Institute, will receive everlasting fame as "Stonewall" Jackson. *Confederate victory.*

July 1861: To thwart the Confederate threat in northern Virginia, a series of earthworks and forts are engineered to surround the City of Washington, adding to protection already offered by active posts such as Fort Washington on the Potomac River.

August 10, 1861: **Battle of Wilson's Creek**, Missouri. The Union Army under General Nathaniel Lyon attacks Confederate troops and state militia southwest of Springfield, Missouri, and, after a disastrous day that includes the death of Lyon, is thrown back. The Confederate victory emphasizes the strong Southern presence west of the Mississippi River. *Confederate victory.*

August 28-29, 1861: Fort Hatteras at Cape Hatteras, North Carolina falls to Union naval forces. This begins the first Union efforts to close southern ports along the Carolina coast. *Union victory.*

September 20, 1861: Lexington, Missouri falls to Confederate forces under Sterling Price. *Confederate victory.*

October 21, 1861: **Battle of Ball's Bluff**, Virginia. Colonel Edward D. Baker, senator from Oregon and a friend of President Lincoln, leads troops across the Potomac River only to be forced back to the river's edge where he is killed. The ensuing Union withdrawal turns into a rout with many soldiers drowning while trying to re-cross the icy waters of the Potomac River. *Confederate victory.*

January 19, 1862: **Battle of Mill Springs**, Kentucky. This *Union victory* weakens the Confederate hold on the state.

February 6, 1862: **Surrender of Fort Henry**, Tennessee. The loss of this Southern fort on the Tennessee River opens the door to Union control of the river. *Union victory.*

February 8, 1862: **Battle of Roanoke Island**, North Carolina. A Confederate defeat, the battle results in Union occupation of eastern

North Carolina and control of Pamlico Sound, to be used as Northern base for further operations against the southern coast. *Union victory*.

February 16, 1862: **Surrender of Fort Donelson**, Tennessee. This capture of the primary Southern fort on the Cumberland River leaves the river in Union hands. It is here that Union General Ulysses S. Grant gained his nickname "Unconditional Surrender." *Union victory*. (Fort Henry and Fort Donelson were the first major Union victories.)

February 22, 1862: Jefferson Davis is inaugurated as President of the Confederate States of America.

March 7-8, 1862: **Battle of Pea Ridge (Elkhorn Tavern)**, **Arkansas.** The Union victory loosens the Confederate hold on Missouri and disrupts southern control of a portion of the Mississippi River. *Union victory*.

March 9, 1862: The naval battle between the USS *Monitor* and the CSS *Virginia* (the old USS *Merrimack*), the first "ironclads," is fought in Hampton Roads, Virginia. *Union victory*.

April 6-7, 1862: **Battle of Shiloh (Pittsburg Landing),** the first major battle in Tennessee. Confederate General Albert Sidney Johnston, a veteran of the Texas War of Independence and the War with Mexico who is considered to be one of the South's finest officers, is killed on the first day of fighting. This *Union victory* further secures the career of Union General Ulysses S. Grant.

April 24-25, 1862: A fleet of Union gunships under Admiral David Farragut passes Confederate forts guarding the mouth of the Mississippi River. On April 25, the fleet arrives at New Orleans, where they demanded the surrender of the city. Within two days the forts fall into Union hands and the mouth of the great river is under Union control. *Union victory.*

May 25, 1862: **First Battle of Winchester**, Virginia. After two weeks of maneuvering and battles at Cross Keys and Front Royal, General "Stonewall" Jackson attacks Union forces at Winchester and successfully drives them from the city. This *Confederate victory* is the culmination of his 1862 Valley Campaign.

May 31-June 1, 1862: **Battle of Seven Pines** near Richmond, Virginia. General Joseph Johnston, commander of the Confederate army in Virginia, is wounded and replaced by Robert E. Lee, who renames his command the Army of Northern Virginia. *Confederate victory.*

June 6, 1862: **Battle of Memphis**, Tennessee. A Union flotilla under Commodore Charles Davis successfully defeats a Confederate river force on the Mississippi River near the city, and Memphis surrenders. The Mississippi River is now in Union control except for its course west of Mississippi where the city of Vicksburg stands as the last Southern stronghold on the great river. *Union victory.*

June 25-July 1, 1862: **Seven Days' Battles** before Richmond. General Lee's army attacks the Army of the Potomac under General George McClellan in a succession of battles beginning at Mechanicsville on June 26 and ending at Malvern Hill on July 1. *Confederate victory*.

August 30-31, 1862: **Battle of Second Bull Run (or Second Manassas)** is fought on the same ground where one year before the Union army was defeated and sent reeling in retreat to Washington. Likewise, the result of this battle is a *Confederate victory*.

September 17, 1862: **Battle of Antietam (Sharpsburg)**, Maryland, the bloodiest single day of the Civil War. The result of the battle ends General Lee's first invasion of the North. *Union victory*.

September 22, 1862: Following the Union victory at Antietam, President Lincoln introduces the Emancipation Proclamation, an executive order that frees every slave in the Confederate States. The Emancipation Proclamation will go into effect on January 1, 1863.

October 8, 1862: Battle of Perryville.

CHAPTER 5

War Strategies

In one respect, the Union and Confederacy had the same goal: to preserve a way of life. But all similarities ended there because both sides wanted a different way of life preserved.

Confederate Strategy

The Confederacy's goal was to secure independence from the North and establish an independent nation free from Northern political oppression and the repression of slavery. In the mind of many Rebels (particularly the political leaders and slave owners) the war was a noble crusade of democracy for white people. This goal was grounded in the belief that the Constitution protected slavery but that the Union had the intention to abolish the tradition. Southerners, therefore, thought they had the right to secede, as it was the only way to defend the institution of slavery and their belief in states' rights. However, it is important to note that a very small minority of Southerners owned slaves. The majority of Confederate soldiers who fought in the Civil War did so for a variety of reasons that might have included the desire to protect their way of life, which happened to include slavery. There were other reasons. During a battle that took place in the Deep South, a Rebel soldier was captured. A Union

sergeant who took the prisoner asked, "Why are you fighting us?'
The Confederate answered, "Because you're down here."

To be victorious, the Confederacy knew it did not need to invade the
North or capture a mile of its territory. Its strategy were fairly
simple:

- Defend Confederate land.
- Prevent the North from destroying the Confederate army.
- Break the Union's will to fight.

Union Strategy

President Lincoln's initial goal was to reconcile the Union. Later, the
objective changed to reuniting the states into a country without
slavery. This intention was based on the belief that the South had no
right to secede from the Union and that secession was treasonous
and an act of rebellion against the Union. Initially, the Union's
strategy was defensive because it did not yet have the soldiers to
wage an offensive into the South after the Rebels fired on Fort
Sumter.

However, after secessionist forces fired on Fort Sumter, President
Abraham Lincoln called for 75,000 volunteers to stop the Southern
rebellion. When Lincoln asked Kentucky to supply four regiments,
Governor Beriah Magoffin refused, stating, "I say, emphatically,

Kentucky will furnish no troops for the wicked purpose of subduing her sister Southern states." Although he supported slavery and the legality of secession, Magoffin worked to keep Kentucky neutral in a failed attempt to broker a peaceful compromise between the North and South. After Kentucky declared neutrality, Magoffin tangled with Lincoln over several issues, including Union enlistments and the military arrests of Kentucky civilians. Neutrality crumbled within four months, however, and Magoffin was left to lead Kentucky—a divided border state—as Union and Confederate troops maneuvered for control of the commonwealth.

The Union's goal eventually changed. When it became clear to Lincoln that the North might lose the war, he changed the purpose for fighting. Freeing the slaves became the reason. Thus, the new Union goal was to retain and reshape the Union by reuniting the states in country that no longer tolerated slavery.

The union developed the Anaconda Plan, which had five primary goals:

- Invade the Confederate States and destroy its will to resist.
- Secure the Mississippi River and cut the Confederacy in half.
- Construct and maintain a naval blockade of 3,500 miles of Confederate coastline.
- Obtain the loyalty of the border states, which included Maryland, Missouri, Kentucky, Delaware, and, in 1863, West Virginia.
- Prevent European powers—especially Great Britain and

France—from extending recognition of and giving assistance to the Confederacy

In 1862 Maryland, Missouri, and Kentucky were neutral in the war and offered an opportunity for the Confederacy. Aggressive military action could result in recognition and European intervention on the side of the Confederates. Victory in the border states would also provide the South valuable resources like men and access to means of transportation via railroads and rivers.

The Battle of Pea Ridge in March 1862 resulted in a Confederate defeat and any chance of winning over Missouri. The same held for Maryland with a strategic Union victory over General Robert E. Lee at Antietam in September 17, 1862. Only Kentucky remained as the last chance for the Confederacy to secure a key geographic and political advantage.

While Kentucky was the only border state that was not fully controlled by the Union, it had opened its borders to Union troops and recruitment following the battle of Belmont and Columbus in November 1861. However, there was still significant support for the Confederacy. For the Union to achieve the last two objectives of its strategy, Kentucky had to be won.

CHAPTER 6
Prelude to the Battle

The Invasion of Kentucky

"I think to lose Kentucky is nearly the same as to lose the whole game. Kentucky gone, we cannot hold Missouri, nor Maryland. These all against us, and the job on our hands is too large for us. We would as well consent to separation at once, including the surrender of this capitol." *Abraham Lincoln, September 1861*

Kentucky was strategically important to both the North and South. The commonwealth ranked ninth in population by 1860 and was a major producer of such agricultural commodities as tobacco, corn, wheat, hemp, and flax. The state also had fine horses that were coveted resource, as well as a potential boost in manpower for the Confederate Army. Geographically, Kentucky was important to the South because the Ohio River would provide a defensible boundary along the entire length of the state.

There had been small battles in Kentucky starting in 1861 where the neutrality was violated. The South seized Columbus, Kentucky in September 1861 for control over the Mississippi, as did the Union, under General Grant, in Paducah. Grant also won battles for Forts Donelson and Henry on the Cumberland River in January and

February 1862. There were also Union victories at Mill Springs and Middle Creek, Kentucky. The Confederacy showed some success disrupting the Louisville to Nashville railroad, which was the Union's primary supply line in the region.

In May 1862, Confederate Brigadier General John Hunt Morgan telegraphed Major General Edmund Kirby-Smith in Knoxville, Tennessee from Lexington, Kentucky following his first great raid through the Bluegrass. He reported the capture of 1,200 Federal soldiers (whom he paroled), the acquisition of several hundred horses, and the destruction of massive quantities of supplies. This unnerved Kentucky's Union military government, and President Abraham Lincoln received so many frantic appeals for help that he complained that "they are having a stampede in Kentucky" In the telegraph Morgan sent to Kirby-Smith, Morgan said he was in Lexington and had burned all the bridges between there and Cincinnati. Furthermore, the area was defended by home guards, and he said the sentiments of the populace was such that "If the Confederacy were to enter the State in force, the people would rise up at once and provide an Army of 25,000 men for the Confederacy." This echoed the rhetoric the Confederate government had been hearing from other expatriated Kentuckians such as John C. Breckinridge and Humphrey Marshall. It was exactly what they wanted to hear, but it was not a valid opinion poll.

Lincoln signed the Emancipation Proclamation September 22, 1862 after the Union victory at Antietam, but it did not go into effect until January 1, 1863. A victory in Kentucky and Confederate control of the Bluegrass State could undermine the viability of the Proclamation and still bring Europe into the war on the side of the South.

Confederate President Jefferson Davis gave very vague guidance on the South's invasion of Kentucky other than instructions to install a Confederate governor in Frankfort and a proclamation that was to be read to the people of Kentucky once the state was entered by the Rebels.

The Confederate invading force consisted of four loosely linked commands led by Generals Kirby Smith, Humphrey Marshall, Braxton Bragg, and Earl Van Dorn. No one was assigned as overall in charge, and the generals had their own agendas that were not necessarily aligned. Furthermore, there was no clear objective, purpose, and overall coordinated strategy. Finally, there was a "gentleman's agreement" where there would be a three-pronged attack with Van Dorn on the left, Smith on the right, and Bragg in the center. This would have given the Confederates 50,000 men to conduct the campaign. However, those forces never converged, mostly because each commander had his own idea of how to conduct the battle. No one wanted to surrender the autonomy and central authority of his command.

The Union forces in Kentucky did have unity of command under

Major General Don Carlos Buell's Army of the Ohio. Nevertheless, he had failed to secure a victory at Chattanooga earlier in the year and was relieved of his command as he gathered his forces in Louisville. No one wanted the job, so Buell was reinstated—with firm guidance from Lincoln that he must aggressively conduct the campaign.

In August 1862, the Confederate invasion began with General Kirby Smith moving into the Big Creek Gap. On August 30, Smith won a decisive battle at Richmond, Kentucky and captures Lexington and Frankfort on September 3. He got no further guidance, so he proceeded north to the Ohio River.

Humphrey Marshall entered Kentucky by way of Pound Gap to interdict and destroy the fleeing Federal Cumberland Gap force of Brigadier General George W. Morgan. Marshall did not engage but escorted Morgan to Greenup, Ohio and then cautiously moved his way to Winchester, Kentucky. Marshall had no significant impact in Kentucky.

General Van Dorn never entered Kentucky, focusing his effort in Mississippi and parts of Louisiana.

On September 14, Bragg entered Kentucky and staged at Glasgow with his Army of the Mississippi, which consisted of a right wing commanded by Major General Leonidas Polk and a left wing commanded by Major General William Hardee. Bragg's strength was 16,500 men and 56 cannon. Bragg then moved his forces to Bardstown on September 22.

One of Bragg's clear instructions from Jefferson Davis was to emplace a Confederate governor in Kentucky. As a result he left Bardstown and went to Frankfort to meet General Kirby-Smith on October 4. Bragg met with Kirby-Smith, and it was agreed that Bragg would assume command of the combined forces in Kentucky and oversee the inauguration of Richard Hawes as the Confederate governor. With Hawes in office the thought was the Confederate Conscription Act would be legitimatized and soldiers could be drafted. This was necessary because the promised Confederate volunteers had not materialized.

General Buell sent two divisions to Frankfort as a feint to deceive the Confederates, which caused Bragg and Smith to vacate the capital, leaving it to the Union. Buell sent the remainder of his force towards Bardstown and Perryville.

Buell had three corps under his command: I Corps led by Major General Alexander McDowell McCook, II Corps led by Major General Thomas Crittenden, and III Corps led by Major General Charles Gilbert. The Army of Ohio had 55,261 men and 147 cannons.

As Union forces arrived in the vicinity of Perryville on October 7, Buell decided to wait until he had all his corps set before battle. He directed the attack take place on October 9.

Going into the battle Buell and Bragg grossly miscalculated the strength of one another's armies. Bragg thought he was facing 22,000 Union troops, and Buell believed the Confederates had 45,000 men. This lack of situational awareness of both commanders contributed to tactical failures during the fight that ensued.

Bragg's army moved toward a concentration with Edmund Kirby-Smith near Versailles, Kentucky. Major General Leonidas Polk's left wing turned north onto the Harrodsburg Pike not far from the town of Perryville and marched to Lawrenceburg. Major General William Hardee, Bragg's right wing commander, was still at Perryville. Hardee halted and sent a message to Major General Bragg regarding the strong Federal force that had annoyed his rear units since leaving Bardstown. Hardee was concerned that should he follow Polk to the North he would uncover the approach to Kirby-Smith's central supply depot, which had been established at Bryantsville some 15 miles northeast of Danville.

In response to Hardee's message Bragg sent this order to Polk:

"General, in view of the news from Hardee you had better move with Cheatham's division to his support and give the enemy battle immediately; rout him and then move to our support at Versailles."

It was Bragg's intention that the fight would start on October 8, the day before Buell wanted to attack.

The Battle of Perryville would soon begin.

Soft Skill Lessons

Many of the decisions made in the prelude to the Battle of Perryville affected the ultimate outcome in the struggle between the North and South on that day. Some of the leaders applied soft skills, and some did not. It is important to remember that solving difficult problems, decision-making, and effectively communicating intent are very important leadership skills.

> ➤ What important communication soft skill did Abraham Lincoln demonstrate with his statement of the importance of Kentucky in the war?
> ➤ What important communication soft skill did Jefferson Davis fail to demonstrate with this guidance to the Army of the Mississippi?
> ➤ With the Army of the Mississippi, what was a possible soft skill shortfall with the relationship between Generals Bragg, Van Dorn, and Smith? What do you think will be a significant impact of this failure?
> ➤ Both Buell and Bragg miscalculated the number of troops in one another's armies. This lack of situational awareness was costly in the upcoming battle. How do you address

challenges "seeing" the strengths and weaknesses of the competition in your business?

Knowing Your Purpose

When I deployed to Iraq in 1991 for Desert Storm, President George H. W. Bush and our military leaders made our purpose very clear: remove the Iraqi Army from Kuwait and restore the international integrity of the invaded country. Similarly, in Bosnia the intent of our operation was well defined: end Serbian genocide of the Bosnian Muslims and separate the former warring factions. In both cases, once the objectives were met, our participation in the conflict was over and we went home.

In the 2003 invasion of Iraq it seemed the reason for the war was precise: overthrow Saddam Hussein and rid Iraq of weapons of mass destruction (WMD). However, when we didn't find WMD, the war morphed into something else. It became a counterinsurgency and, to a degree, an exercise in nation-building. However, it took a very long time for our leaders to recognize the character of the war and articulate it to us. Frankly, it was not until General Petraeus assumed command that the reason we were at war was fully understood.

The format of the Army mission statement during combat operations is very simple. The two most important components are the task and purpose. The task is a very specific assignment that must be attained.

For example, when an organization is told to destroy the enemy it means to render it combat ineffective so they can no longer fight. If they are told to seize a certain terrain feature, they must occupy and control it. If they are told to block, that means the enemy cannot pass or move through an area. The Army actually has a dictionary that provides the precise meaning of each task.

A task must be *definable, attainable*, and *decisive*. We call it DAD in the Army.

The purpose is the reason *why* a task is performed. Of the two parts of a mission statement, the purpose is the most important. A leader can get the task wrong, but a poorly crafted purpose can lead to disaster. On the other hand, a well-constructed purpose statement can unleash tremendous potential in the way of initiative, flexibility, adaptability, and organizational direction.

For example, the mission of my organization during Desert Storm was to block enemy forces moving along Highway 8 to prevent them from repositioning to Baghdad.

The task was block Highway 8, and the purpose was to prevent the enemy from returning to the capitol. Seems simple enough. However, what if we saw the enemy taking a different route within our area of responsibility other than Highway 8? Would we sit on the road and wave at them as they drove along another thoroughfare en route to Baghdad? We were blocking Highway 8 after all. Of course that wouldn't have been acceptable. We would have moved to the other location and block the movement there because we understood the purpose of what we were doing.

In Greg Coker's book, *Building Cathedrals: The Power of Purpose*, he tells the story of three bricklayers who are building a cathedral. The architect who designed the church inquired from one mason what he was doing, and the man answered, "I am laying bricks." He questioned the other, who said, "I am building a wall." The last bricklayer was asked what he was doing, and he answered enthusiastically, "I am building a cathedral."

The last bricklayer knew his purpose precisely.

If you consider the directions given by President Lincoln and Jefferson Davis, who provided the clearest purpose? What is the purpose of your organization? Hint: It's not to sale this or build that.

Who's Who at Perryville

Army of the Ohio

Major General Don Carlos Buell
Commander of the Army of the Ohio

- West Point 1841.

- Fought in Seminole Wars and Mexico, promoted for gallantry.

- Lacked flair, but was a strict disciplinarian and superior administrator and had a strong work ethic.
- Was court martialed as a young officer for whipping a soldier with a sword.
- Was a rigid micromanager and was considered cold and aloof by his subordinates.
- Had little tolerance for politics and particularly politicians who interfered in the war, including President Lincoln,
- Owned eight slaves through marriage but sold them when the war broke out; he was often considered too lenient on the South and was even called a sympathizer.
- Considered war a science and believed a commander should only fight when he has a significant tactical advantage.

Major General Charles Gilbert
Commander, III Corps

- West Point 1846.
- Fought in the Mexican War.
- Was promoted in 1862 from captain to acting major general (four ranks) because several officers refused the position.
- Had never led a unit larger than a company before taking command of the III Corps.

Major General Alexander McDowell McCook
Commander, I Corps

- West Point 1852.

- Fought on the frontier against the Indians.
- Nicknamed "Gutsy" because of his ample waistline, rather than his mettle.
- Described as enthusiastic, empathic, impulsive, and having a heart of gold.

Brigadier General Phillip Henry Sheridan
Commander, 11th Division

- West Point 1853. He graduated 34th of 52 in his class and was suspended a year for threatening to run classmate William Terrill through with a bayonet for an insult on the parade field. (Terrill also fought at Perryville.)
- Fought in the Indian Wars.
- Nicknamed "Little Phil" and "Fighting Phil."
- Promoted to brigadier general after his heroic actions at the Battle of Booneville, Mississippi.

Brigadier General James Jackson
Commander, 10th Division

- Jefferson College 1844
- Kentuckian.
- Lawyer in Hopkinsville, Kentucky before the war.
- Served in the Mexican War as a private and was later promoted to 3rd lieutenant, but resigned after participating in a duel for fear of court martial.

- Elected to Kentucky Congress as Unionist but resigned to enter the Union Army.
- Considered a tyrant, he was hated by his men for his lack of concern for their wellbeing.

Brigadier General William Terrill
Commander, 33rd Brigade

- West Point 1853.
- Served during the 3rd Seminole War.
- From Virginia, volunteered to serve in the Union while his brother chose to serve for the Confederacy. Both were killed while commanding brigades during the war.
- As a captain, commanded a cannon battery at the Battle of Shiloh, where he served with distinction. Six months later he was promoted to brigadier general (three ranks).
- Like his commander, Brigadier General Jackson, was not liked by his soldiers.

Brigadier General Lovell Rousseau
Commander, 3rd Division

- Self-educated
- Kentuckian; father was a slave owner
- Lawyer, Indiana Congressman, and later Kentucky Senator but resigned to serve in the Union.
- Fought in the Mexican War.

- It was said, "No officer in the Army is more beloved than the gallant General Rousseau."

Colonel John Starkweather
Commander, 28th Brigade

- Union College 1850.
- Lawyer; no previous war experience.
- Former commander of the 1st Wisconsin.
- Spoke with familiarity and trust.
- Took care of his men.

Army of the Mississippi

General Braxton Bragg
Commander of the Army of the Mississippi

- West Point 1837.
- Fought in the Mexican War and distinguished himself in several battles.
- As a junior officer, was chronically ill, ill humored, contentious, sarcastic, and tactless. He was court martialed twice.
- In 1862, was considered one of the best-regarded officers in the Confederate Army.
- Had great administrative skills and was a superior logistician and trainer, transforming the Army of the Mississippi from a motley group into an effective fighting force.

- Historians have argued whether he was bipolar, had a narcissistic personality disorder, or was simply insane.

Major General Leonidas Polk
Commander of the Right Wing

- West Point 1827.
- Resigned his commission and was later ordained an Episcopalian bishop and founder of the University of the South.
- Was a classmate of Jefferson Davis and used their friendship to get commissioned a major general and put in command of a corps.
- General Bragg despised Polk, calling him "an old woman and utterly worthless."
- Had the unfortunate habit of disobeying orders.

Major General Benjamin Cheatam
Commander, 1st Division

- Had an accomplished private tutor through boyhood and then several sessions at Nashville Boys Academy followed by several years in the Nashville Blues Militia, where he was voted lieutenant.
- Father and maternal grandfather were both distinguished military men from whom Cheatham got personal tutorage in the arts of war.
- Born to a prominent plantation family in Tennessee.

- Served in the Mexican War, where he entered as a captain and left as a colonel.
- Participated in the 1849 Gold Rush.
- Not liked by Bragg, who considered him a ruffian with no military abilities.
- Bragg wanted to remove him from command, but Cheatham was very popular with his Tennessee troops.
- Known for his consumption of alcohol.

Brigadier General Daniel Donelson
Commander, Donelson's Brigade

- West Point 1825.
- Resigned commission to become a planter.
- No prior war experience before the Civil War.
- Elected to the Tennessee House of Representatives.
- Was accused by subordinates for being a drunk.
- Nephew of Andrew Jackson.

Colonel John Savage
Commander, 16th Tennessee

- Saint Mary's College, Lebanon, Kentucky.
- Served in the Seminole Wars as a private.
- Became a lawyer before the Civil War.
- Arrested and court martialed by Donelson for not obeying orders, but the legal action was dropped; however, the relationship between the two was strained.

Brigadier General George Maney
Commander, Maney's Brigade

- Attended Nashville Seminary and later graduated from University of Nashville in 1845 at the age of 19.

- Served in the Mexican War.

- Lawyer and elected to the Tennessee State Legislature before the war.

Brigadier General Alexander Stewart
Commander, Stewart's Brigade

- West Point 1842.

- Resigned his commission to become a professor of mathematics and experimental philosophy at Cumberland University and later University of Nashville.

- Though he was a strong anti-secessionist Whig politically, accepted a commission as a major in the Tennessee militia.

Soft Skill Lessons

➤ Based on the information provided, rank order the leaders you think will be most effective.

➤ How does education and experience play a part in your selection?

CHAPTER 7
The Battle of Perryville

Got Water?

Disease and lack of water, not musket or cannon fire, were the greatest killers on the Civil War battlefield. As mentioned earlier, the summer and autumn of 1862 brought a great drought across the Appalachian Mountains and the Midwest. Water was so scarce that men would take it from about any source regardless of its purity. Men were constantly dehydrated and became sick. The problem was made worse by the long marches and lack of good food.

One of the reasons General Braxton Bragg chose Perryville to fight was because of decent water that could be found in the Chaplin River and the creeks in the area. General Don Carlos Buell was in hot pursuit of the Confederate Army and started to take positions along the rolling hills to prepare for battle. Bragg ordered Major General Leonidas Polk to stop, secure the water, and eliminate the Federal threat. Bragg wanted a deliberate and coordinated attack on October 8. Buell wanted to properly position his forces and begin the battle on October 9.

During the early predawn hours of October 8 near Peters Hill on the Union right flank, newly promoted Brigadier General P.H. Sheridan was sent forward to secure access to a water source. Peters Hill was a dominating terrain feature that allowed control of the Dixville Crossroads and the main approach to the town of Perryville. Confederate Division Commander Brigadier General S.B. Buckner had placed two regiments of Brigadier General St. John Liddell's brigade on Peters Hill. Buckner placed the remainder of that brigade on Bottoms Hill a half mile to the east. Around midnight Federal cavalry scouts were engaged at Bottoms Hill and again on Peters Hill as they withdrew. Sheridan then attacked Peters Hill with a brigade and drove Liddell's men off. However, the Rebels mounted a successful counterattack. Sheridan attacked again with three brigades and artillery support. The Confederates retreated, and the Union gained control of both Peters and Bottoms Hills. This skirmish ended around 10 o'clock in the morning.

Buckner understood that Peters and Bottom Hills were important to the defense of the crossroads in Perryville but that holding them would require more men. Buckner deferred the decision to Major General Leonidas Polk, who had arrived with Franklin Cheatham's Division. Polk decided to let the positions go and ordered his brigades to establish new defensive lines along the banks of the Chaplin River.

As Sheridan secured Peters and Bottom Hills, Major General Don Carlos Buell was having breakfast with Major General Charles Gilbert at his headquarters three miles west of Peters Hill. Buell heard faint cannon fire from Sheridan's artillery. Buell had been injured the previous day when he was thrown from his horse. Unable to ride, Buell instructed Gilbert to go forward and instruct Sheridan to "not do anything that would bring about a general engagement before all three corps were in line and to stop that useless waste of gunpowder." Gilbert found Sheridan on Bottoms Hill and reported, "He was astounded to find him (Sheridan) so far forward of his assigned position." Gilbert reprimanded Sheridan and ordered him to return to Peters Hill, dig in, and await further orders. Gilbert then returned to Buell's headquarters, where he was invited to stay for brandy and dinner.

As Sheridan moved his division back to Peters Hill, Major General Braxton Bragg rode to Perryville from his headquarters in Harrodsburg to find out why Polk had not given battle as ordered. Bragg was upset over Polk's insubordination. He directed Polk to deploy his cavalry and determine the disposition of the Federal force. The cavalry identified elements of Brigadier General Lovell Rousseau's division approaching the Mackville Road northwest of Peters Hill. The Union seemed to be consolidating their forces near the strategically important Dixville Crossroads. However, Bragg was still convinced that Buell's main body was near Frankfort. He thought the unit pursuing Major General Hardee was no more than a corps (about 10,000 men). Nevertheless, he assumed the Federals' intent at Peters Hill was to outflank him. Bragg orders Cheatham's division to move north of the newly arriving Union regiments and attack "without further delay."

Sheridan's lack of good situational awareness brought about the general engagement. Gilbert then gave away the ground gained rather than bringing the III and I Corps into a solid line. He left the flank of I Corps open for exploitation while at the same time rendering all of III Corps ineffective.

Soft Skill Lessons

- ➢ How are you, as a leader, prepared to address inevitable friction within your organization?
- ➢ Are you and is your organization flexible and adaptable enough to react to situations when things don't go as planned?
- ➢ What are the soft skills that can better prepare you and your organization for the fog and friction that is a natural aspect of your work?

Fog and Friction

Both Generals Bragg and Buell had very specific intentions on how the battle was to begin. However, fate and circumstance caused the situation to unfold in an unexpected way. This would have a significant effect later in the day when the soldiers became engaged in combat. The clash started over the desire to secure a scarce resource. The lack of water and the search for it resulted in the premature initiation of hostilities.

The Napoleonic-era military writer and philosopher Carl Von Clausewitz wrote, "In war more than anywhere else things do not turn out as we expect. Nearby they do not appear as they did from a distance." This vignette is a foreshadowing of events to come, where chance and friction play a significant role in the outcome of many encounters of the day. Some schools of thought assert that there is nothing that can be done about the friction and the fog of war. The belief is that you just react to it. However, leadership styles often either lessen or contribute to the adverse effect of chance circumstances. Great leaders leverage the fog and friction of war to their advantage.

Consider the personalities of the two commanding generals.

General Braxton Bragg was impulsive and often reckless. He was also ill humored and contentious. As a junior officer, Bragg was court martialed twice. Some historians say he was bipolar or even insane. There is a story that General U.S. Grant told of Bragg when they served together before the war. Bragg was both a company commander and the unit supply officer. According to Grant, Bragg would write a request for supplies for his unit as the company commander and then disapprove them as the logistics officer. Now, that is kind of crazy.

General Don Carlos Buell, on the other hand, was rigid, and his decision-making was very deliberate. He believed everything had to be set perfectly before conducting an operation. He often experienced "paralysis by analysis." He was also very confident of his abilities—so much so that he often publicly challenged Abraham Lincoln on the President's policies because they did not align with his own. Lincoln, on other hand, believed Buell was not aggressive enough and too slow carrying out his orders. When Buell failed in the Tennessee campaign several months before Perryville because of a lack of aggressiveness, Lincoln fired him. Without options for a replacement, Lincoln was forced to reinstate Buell before the invasion of Kentucky.

Clearly, Bragg and Buell had contrasting leadership styles that were on the extremes of rash and rigid. For a leader to be effective, there has to be a middle ground.

If you carefully watch military movies about the wars in Iraq and Afghanistan, you may notice how soldiers clear rooms. Take the film *Zero Dark Thirty* about the raid that killed Osama Bin Laden. The SEALS conducting the operation didn't just rush into the building and start firing at everything that moved. Their movements were very deliberate, but at the same time they had a sense of urgency. This is called *being in a careful hurry*. In close quarters combat, the mantra is *slow is smooth, smooth is fast*. However, when contact is made with the enemy you attack with *violence of action.* This is a mental process that soldiers are repeatedly trained in until it becomes ingrained in their psyche.

In July 2007 the brigade that I was assigned attacked and took control of the city of Baqubah. I was working with the Iraqi forces to take a convoy down to Baghdad, which was about 60 miles away. As we were completing final preparations, I saw a young Iraqi man walking briskly towards us with an intense look in his eyes. I saw a bulge in his loose, untucked shirt.

Suicide belt, I thought.

I unholstered my 9mm and pointed it at him. I shouted in Arabic for him to stop and lie down, but he kept moving. I shouted again, this time in English: "Damn it, get down!"

He stopped, raised his hands, and in very good English replied: "It's okay, I'm a policeman! I'm here to help!" I told him to raise his shirt. He did, exposing a pistol—which I then found out had no bullets in it. Akmed, as he introduced himself, said he knew how to get to the place where we going in Baghdad. Akmed accompanied us on the mission and he presence largely contributed to our success.

I nearly shot Akmed. My first inclination was to pull the trigger, and I probably would have if he continued to move forward. However, my training had taught me *not to rush to failure.*

As it pertains to business, how does *being in a careful hurry* and *not rushing to failure* reduce the adverse effects of fog and friction that is inherent in both war and the workplace? What are the instances where *slow is smooth and smooth is fast*? And what conditions must be present to execute a task with *violence of action*?

Do You Hear What I Hear?

General Buell moved down from Louisville and established his headquarters about four miles from where the battle took place. The hills were rolling throughout the area of operations. The wind was also blowing steadily away from where Buell was positioned. This caused an atmospheric effect called an *acoustic shadow*, which allowed Buell to hear only faint sounds of the large guns and almost none of the muskets. Buell didn't know the battle had started until it was almost over. He was overconfident and believed the attack would not start until he ordered it to begin the next day, October 9.

When Sheridan unintentionally initiated the battle on the early morning of October 8, Buell instructed Major General Charles Gilbert to ride out and tell Sheridan to "stop wasting good powder." The acoustic shadow prevented Buell from knowing the intensity of the fighting. The Union commander didn't understand the battle had started for all practical purposes. Gilbert did as he was told, instructed Sheridan to fall back, giving up valuable ground and then returned. But he did not explain the actual situation to his boss.

Buell did not like to hear bad news and Gilbert certainly wasn't going to deliver it. But why?

Major General "Bull" Nelson had been the III Corps Commander. Nelson was a very effective leader. Unfortunately, a fellow officer killed him with a pistol after a dispute at the Galt Hotel in Louisville just days before the battle.

Buell asked several men to assume command of III Corps. All the men he asked had attended West Point because Buell believed that West Pointers were superior leaders. However, there were two other officers who were very effective and wanted the job but hadn't attended West Point. Instead of choosing the better leaders, Buell opted to promote Captain Charles Gilbert, a West Point graduate, to major general and assign him to command III Corps.

Gilbert jumped five ranks from captain to major general. He had never led an organization larger than 200 men and now he was responsible for 20,000. Major General Gilbert stayed near Buell for most of the Battle of Perryville. Very few men of Gilbert's corps got into the fight.

Soft Skill Lessons

> Is there an acoustic shadow in your organization? Do you personally have an acoustic shadow?

- Are people comfortable telling you bad news? How well do you accept it?
- Do you surround yourself with people who tell you what you *want* to hear or what you *need* to hear?
- Do you promote people based on competence or do you advance employees simply because you like them?
- What are the soft skills that would help prevent you from creating an acoustic shadow in your organization?

Acoustic Shadows

In 1993 David Petraeus took our battalion to the National Training Center (NTC) for a two-week exercise. The NTC replicates combat scenarios in a desert environment against a very capable opposing force comprised of some of the best leaders and soldiers in the Army. It is a very real simulation of war and possibly the hardest training that I ever participated in.

Our battalion had been given the mission to take control of an area from the enemy, who had mined and placed obstacles to impede the armored attack of another friendly unit. The success of the entire operation was dependent on our ability to secure the location. The battalion operations officer was a major and developed the plan. He briefed Petraeus along with myself and four other company commanders. We would have to lead our soldiers to accomplish the task. The major outranked everyone but Petraeus, and he made that fact very clear to all of us on more than one occasion.

The operations officer proposed a strategy where the battalion would move by foot through a very narrow valley called the Goat Trail. During the brief, he displayed the suspected enemy locations along the route. The company commanders couldn't believe what he showed us. The passageway was filled with opposing force locations. It would have been suicide.

The company commanders stepped back from the briefing table and looked at one another like *what the hell*. Petraeus saw our dismay and asked, "What's wrong company commanders?"

We kept quiet because we feared the wrath of the major when the battalion commander wasn't around. Finally Petraeus said, "Damn it, commanders, what's on your minds? We don't have time to mess around."

We jointly expressed our concerns about the direction of attack because of the density of enemy forces. My fellow company commanders and I had talked before the briefing about where we believed the best approach would be and now showed Petraeus and the operations officer. The course of action we proposed was risky because it required the battalion to climb a steep and rocky escarpment. However, we would totally bypass the enemy and attack them from the rear of their position.

Petraeus liked the idea and went with it. The plan worked all the way up to the point we reached our final location. The opposing force called indirect fire on us, and we capitulated. Nonetheless, we accomplished our mission. However, as we consolidated our forces, no one could find Petraeus.

I finally located him near the top of a small mountain where we had attacked. He was there cheering on the force that was moving through the breach we helped create. He pumped his fists in the air and yelled, "Go get 'em, Olson," referring to his West Point classmate who was leading the mechanized offensive.

Our purpose was to help open the breach. We did that even though most of us were "simulated" casualties. Nonetheless, the ultimate success of the mission was to help enable the armored attack. Petraeus rooted his buddy on to the final objective. He understood the purpose of our mission.

One of the best ways to eliminate acoustic shadows in your organization is engaging your employees and subordinate leaders to gain a fresh perspective. It takes courage for a leader to do that. The boss is supposed to know everything, right? The good ones realize they don't. The great ones know the difference between sound advice and a bad recommendation. There is also the advantage of employee buy in. People always work harder when they are a part of the problem-solving discussion.

Now You See it, Now you Don't

Before the main battle began, Major General Benjamin Franklin Cheatham, the Confederate division commander in Major General Leonidas Polk's right wing, readied his 8,000 men for combat. He was to lead the opening attack. Cheatham had three brigades under his command led by Brigadier General Daniel Donelson, Brigadier General George Maney, and Brigadier General Alexander Stewart. Each brigade would play an important role in the day's events.

The Confederates conducted a reconnaissance hours before the start of the battle. During the patrol, the cavalry drove off Union troops forward of the slope of a hill in the direction of the Rebels' intended attack. However, they stopped short of going beyond the hill.

As a result, they failed to see a much superior Union force forming over a mile in length along the full width of the ridgeline. The rolling hills created an optical illusion. The cavalry could see one ridgeline but not the others because of the deceptive terrain. They reported what they saw back to Major General Cheatham.

Even though reports indicated that Buell had potentially three corps converging on Perryville, Bragg still believe that he outnumbered the Union forces. Confident he had greater force, and with the urging of Bragg, Major General Cheatham ordered Brigadier General Donelson to attack the Federals to his front. Donelson had 970 men at the time because Cheatham had detached units from the brigade to other locations on the battlefield.

What neither of the two commanders understood was the Union had 5,200 soldiers defending the hills to the front of them. Moreover, the Confederates thought they were attacking the Union flank, which is an area of weakness that can be exploited. However, they were actually attacking the Federals' center and their strength.

Soft Skill Lessons

➢ What are the potential *optical illusions* that may delude you and or your organization?

➢ How do you prevent *optical illusions* from deceiving you?

➢ What soft skill helps avert falling into the traps *optical illusions* may present?

Optical Illusions

When I was in Iraq in 2007, I was on a four-vehicle convoy in the Shia-held east side of Baghdad. The fact the area was predominantly Shia was important because the enemy forces from that religious sect had a unique and very lethal type of roadside bomb called the Explosive Formed Projectile or EFP. The EFP shot very hot steel at a high rate of speed that could tear through most any armor we had on our vehicles. During the patrol, we approached a solitary refreshment kiosk in the middle of an isolated city block. Usually local residents would fill the streets and sidewalks, but none were in sight. Soft drink cans were placed in neat rows on the stand's shelf, but no one was present at the stand to sell the items. It was an anomaly that signaled trouble. However, before we could react the vehicle directly to my rear of my truck was hit by an EFP. The sound was like lightning striking right next to you. I can still hear it.

Smoke billowed from the disabled vehicle. The hatch had to be manually let down. When it was finally opened, soldiers emerged from inside like ghosts in a mist-filled cemetery. The smoke was from a signaling grenade that had exploded. The faces of the occupants were coated in a white film that reminded me of pictures of people who were near the World Trade Center towers on 9/11 and who were covered with the dust from the buildings that had collapsed. One soldier in the vehicle received a serious leg wound from the shrapnel, but he later recovered. The other men and women were unharmed physically, although some still carry the emotional wounds from the attack.

We later learned that the EFP was hidden behind the kiosk. The refreshment stand represented an optical illusion to us. We were lured into a false sense of safety when our alert posture should have been heightened.

It is easy to be deceived when we don't proactively question things that appear out of the ordinary like the kiosk—we knew something was wrong but we didn't act on it fast enough.

In the case of Bragg and Cheatham, they didn't trust reports the Union had far more men available than those visible on the hill. The combined effects of the physical terrain, a lack of thorough reconnaissance, and overconfidence created an optical illusion.

They both fell into the trap of believing what they wanted to be true, rather than finding out the actual truth. They trusted an inaccurate version of reality.

Knowing the competitor's, strengths and weaknesses is at the very core of problem solving. It is the start point for determining courses of actions to beat business adversaries, no different than an enemy combatant. Systems must be in place to confirm or deny optical illusions that can blur an organization's vision and undermine effectiveness.

Into the Valley of Death Walked the 970

General Braxton Bragg directed Major General Polk to initiate the main attack with Cheatham's Division at daylight on the morning of October 8. Polk dismissed the order and didn't bother to inform his superior. There had been a long history between Bragg and his subordinate leader. There was a toxic environment of distrust and tension. It was well known that Bragg did not like either Polk or Cheatham. He called Polk "an old woman who was utterly worthless" and thought Cheatham was an incompetent drunk.

Bragg's headquarters was about 20 miles away in the town of Harrodsburg. When he woke that morning, Bragg couldn't hear the sounds of battle so he rode to Perryville to find out what was happening. When Bragg arrived, he chose to assume responsibility for battle preparations himself. He did this without a full appreciation for the status of both the enemy forces and his own troops. It's unclear whether Bragg knew or cared that Donelson's brigade was severely short-handed and only had 970 of his normally assigned 2,000. Moreover, Donelson did not have immediate artillery support.

Even with this lack of knowledge, Bragg ordered the attack and Cheatham directed Brigadier General Donelson to commence the assault.

Donelson focused his assault on a single artillery battery on a hill, which he believed to be the Union flank and a point of weakness. However, unbeknownst to him it was the Federal center and a position of strength. Donelson ordered Colonel John Savage, to lead the attack with his 370 soldiers of the 16th Tennessee.

Donelson and Savage had a turbulent history. First, Donelson was a heavy drinker and Savage was a teetotaler, which caused some friction. Second, Donelson unsuccessfully attempted to court martial Savage for repeatedly disobeying orders. Finally, soldiers loved Donelson and despised Savage, which caused discontent in the ranks.

When Donelson orders the attack, Savage refuses because he thought Donelson was drunk and was ordering him to his death. Savage told his boss, "General, I will obey your orders, but if the 16th (his regiment) is to charge that battery you must give the order." In other words, Savage would not be responsible for the deaths of his men. He wanted his commander to shoulder that burden. Donelson then shouted "Charge!" and the main battle began.

As Savage began the assault, he started to receive fire from two other locations. It was something straight out of Lord Alfred Tennyson's *The Charge of the Light Brigade.* There was literally "cannon to right of them, cannon to left of them, cannon in front of them." However, instead of 600 riding into the valley of death, 970 walked into it and met a similar fate as the Light Brigade. Donelson and his men were torn to shreds.

The poem *The Charge of the Light Brigade* is based on the actual 1854 Battle of Balaclava between the British and the Russians during the Crimean War. The British Cavalry met a nearly the same fate as Donelson's brigade for very similar reasons. Both commanders failed to understand the strength and disposition of the enemy they faced.

Soft Skill Lessons

➤ How did the relationships between commanders affect conduct of the battle?

➤ Donelson was designated the main effort for the attack, but he had only 60 percent of his brigade and did not have artillery support.

➤ Leaders are supposed to set their employees up for success. How and why did the entire chain of command from Bragg to Donelson fail Colonel Savage and his men?

The Main Effort

In Army operations, a single unit is designated as the main effort to accomplish the larger organization's overall mission. Supporting efforts are identified to enable the main effort's success. In the case of Cheatham's attack, Donelson was the main effort for the division and Savage was the main effort for the brigade. This continues all the way down to the lowest level.

A modern day combat imperative is: *designate, sustain and shift the main effort*. This provides the priority of resources and flexibility to assign another unit as the main effort if it looks like the mission might fail. Cheatham clearly selected Donelson as the main effort, but he did not provide the resources and supporting units to help ensure success. We will see later that Cheatham shifted his main effort, but only after Donelson's Brigade had been nearly destroyed.

During my second tour in Iraq in 2007, our brigade was tasked to attack the city of Baqubah. Baqubah was the capitol of Diyala Province and had a population of over 200,000 people. Al Qaeda had seized control of the town and had established strict Sharia law, which included executions, school closings, subjugation of women, and denial of some essential services.

The main effort for the attack was a battalion of over 600 soldiers. Their mission was to clear a portion of the town where most of the terrorists had secured a foothold. Supporting efforts isolated the area to prevent the enemy from escaping. Artillery and air support targeted key known Al Qaeda locations, and engineers cleared routes of mines and booby traps. The main effort battalion was given a single task and purpose, and everyone else was responsible for enabling their success.

I was a supporting effort, but I had a very nontraditional task and purpose, one that had nothing to do with killing the enemy. My mission was to help restore essential services like food, water, electricity and sewage to increase the quality of life for the townspeople. My boss believed that our first priority must be destroying Al Qaeda but the citizen's wellbeing had to get better or we were no different than the terrorists.

A few days after our attack, I went to Baqubah's City Hall to meet the mayor and develop a plan to restore essential services. I really had no idea where to begin and hoped he would have some ideas.

Baqubah's mayor was Abdullah Abdullah (yes, he had the same first and last name). Abdullah was a short, well-dressed man who reminded me a lot of Danny DeVito, except he had a full and meticulously maintained head of hair. I referred to Abdullah as *Sidi*, an Arabic term of respect. He called me *Johnson* because Fred was too difficult. When he was excited, he would say my name several times in a row: *Johnson-Johnson-Johnson!*

Abdullah's office had one desk and one chair, and it was always full of very unhappy citizens. The scene somewhat resembled a Wall Street trading floor just before the closing bell, except here old men with turbans, young men in suits, and even a few women in hijabs screamed their grievances over everything from the lack of electricity to the sewage in the streets.

The crowd engulfed Abdullah. His head would appear and disappear from view, bobbing in the sea of the mob as though he were a buoy in rough waters. I raised my arms halfway up from my sides, palms up. *What in the hell are we going to do?* I wondered. The mayor emerged from the horde soaked in sweat and pulled me to a side room. Abdullah looked around, put one finger to his mouth to shush me, and said, "Johnson-Johnson," pulling me towards a corner of the room farther away from the crowd.

Then he explained to me, among other things, that he'd been a bus driver before becoming mayor. "I'm the only person that would take the job," he told me. "I'm not sure what we should do."

Perfect, I thought. I can't change the oil in my car, let alone fix the electrical grid of a city, and the guy in charge of that city is a bus driver. We were Humpty and Dumpty with no clue how to put Baqubah back together again.

With the promise to meet again the next day, the crowd dispersed in small groups until everyone was gone.

Abdullah slumped in his chair. I pulled up several crates next to the mayor and sat with him. He signaled to his only assistant to bring chai—simple black tea in this case. After letting the steaming cups cool a couple minutes, Abdullah took a sip and winced. I asked him what was wrong. He said, "No sugar. So bitter."

Staff Sergeant Jared Knapp, the leader of my personal security detachment, was listening. Knapp went out to our vehicle and came back with several packets of sugar. When he came back in, he extended them to Abdullah, and Abdullah looked as if Knapp had just offered him a bar of gold. But Abdullah did not take the sugar; he folded the packets gently back into Knapp's hand and pushed them away. "Thank you, but I can't take these," he said.

I laughed. "Why?" I asked. "It's just a couple packets of sugar."

Abdullah's face turned grim. He said, "We haven't had sugar for months. I know one thing about being mayor, and that is that if I take the sugar, there would be a riot." He told us that Al Qaeda controlled the warehouses that had the supplemental food items (like sugar) that citizens normally got from the government.

Abdullah continued: "Saddam Hussein implemented the food distribution system to counter the effects of the economic sanctions of the First Gulf War." The program of Hussein's he described sounded a lot like the WIC system for low-income families in the U.S. Abdullah sighed, then said, "Iraqis became dependent on the government rations. When Al Qaeda seized the warehouses, they used food as a weapon to control the population. The Trade Ministry in Baghdad stopped transporting food to Baqubah because it was not safe. The warehouses here are nearly empty now."

I asked what other items were part of their usual supplement. In addition to sugar, it included food items like rice, dry milk, and flour. The mayor drew a shaky breath and said, defeated, "If we could only get Baghdad to start shipping the food again. That would keep the people off my back for a while so we can figure out what to do with the water, electricity, and sewage."

A look of epiphany flashed onto Staff Sergeant Knapp's face. He took the sugar packets back out of his pockets, one in each hand. He brought the two together into one hand, and as he did he said, "Well, why don't *we* go down to Baghdad, get the food, and bring it back here to Baqubah?"

Abdullah and I had been staring blindly into the abyss. Knapp's suggestion snapped our heads upright. Abdullah and I locked eyes, then smiled and nodded at each other. We had identified our main effort—food.

Carl Von Clausewitz once said, "War is very simple, but the simplest things in war are very difficult." He was right a hundred times over in Iraq, a thousand times over in Baqubah.

Getting food from Baghdad to Baqubah was one of the most difficult missions I faced during that deployment. Once we did, though, there was a remarkable increase in the citizens' morale and faith in us.

With a steady flow of food into the city we shifted our main effort to water, electricity, and sewage. It didn't all get done before we left, but significant progress was made.

Do you designate, sustain and, when necessary, shift main efforts in your organization? Do you precisely assign tasks to your supporting efforts?

Move to the Sound of the Guns

The artillery that was causing the greatest damage to Donelson was on a small hill called the Open Knob that was about one mile away to the right front of his brigade. Major General Cheatham had both

George Maney and Alexander Stewart's brigades that had not been engaged yet. The initial plan was for Stewart to support Donelson's attack. However, Cheatham became so absorbed with the devastating effects of the artillery that he failed to order Stewart to move. Stewart watched as Donelson's men got slaughtered, but he didn't budge.

When later asked why he did not come to the assistance of his fellow commander Stewart said he had not been ordered to do so.

Cheatham finally ordered Brigadier General George Maney to destroy the enemy battery on the Open Knob. He told Maney, "Press with all practicality to the sound of Parson's guns." (Lieutenant Charles Parson was the commander of the artillery battery that was inflicting so much damage on Donelson's brigade.)

Brigadier General Maney had 2,000 men in his brigade. He moved them in a line that stretches nearly one mile along a small valley that provided some protection from cannon and musket fire. To their front was the Open Knob with Parson's artillery battery of eight cannons. A brigade of several thousand men, led by Brigadier General William Terrill, protected the hill. The Division Commander, Brigadier General James Jackson, was located there as well because it was the furthest left flank of the Union and one of the most decisive points on the battlefield.

The Open Knob was a formidable position for Maney to attack. It

The Open Knob was a formidable position for Maney to attack. It was made even more daunting by a fence that ran across the entire width of the battlefield. There was no way to get around it. The barrier would be particularly difficult to breach because it was overgrown with vegetation, creating a wall nearly the height of a man. The obstacle was very similar to the hedgerows of the Second World War that the Allied Forces encountered. The Confederate troops had to go over it or through it in the face of intense fire.

Maney ordered the attack, but the brigade was stalled at the fence. The fence provided *concealment* so the exact location of the Confederate soldiers couldn't be seen, but it didn't afford *cover* to protect the men from the withering fire of the Union troops on the Open Knob. The distance to the top of the hill was a mere 200 yards. However, the Rebels were being engaged with both musket fire and canister from the cannons. Canister consisted of several dozen ball-bearing-sized projectiles that are sprayed like a shotgun at the attacking force. These munitions could penetrate straight through into Maney's troops who are hiding behind the fence because they didn't have *cover*. Soldiers were being shot as they tried to climb over or squirm through openings in the obstacle.

At some point, Maney turned to his aide Thomas Malone and asked, "What do you think we should do?" Malone responded, "I don't think our position can be maintained, and our only chance is to take the guns." Maney then asked Malone if he thought they could do it and Malone replied, "I think so." Maney mounted his horse and rode the length of the formation commanding, "Take those guns."

The soldiers climbed over the fence line and began the assault.

Soft Skill Lessons

- ➤ Compare Maney's action during his attack with Stewart's inaction to support Donelson. What soft skill did Maney exhibit and Stewart lack?
- ➤ Consider Cheatham's order to Maney, "Press with all practicality to the sound of Parson's guns." There's no historical evidence that Maney had much more guidance than that from his boss. What soft skill did Maney exhibit?
- ➤ In the heat of battle, Maney turned to his much more junior aide and essentially asked, "What should I do?" Some people may think that is a weakness, but how can it be a strength? What lessons are there for leadership and followership?
- ➤ Cover provides protection from harm; concealment hides you from it. If you confuse the two it can be devastating. How does the idea of cover and concealment relate to your workplace?
- ➤ How do you overcome obstacles? Why is personal courage so important in leading your employees over or through barriers to achieve mission success.

Initiative

A Message to Garcia was required reading when I was a junior officer. It is a very short pamphlet written by Elbert Hubbard in 1899 at the time of the Spanish American War. The story is about Lieutenant Andrew S. Rowan, who was given a letter by President William McKinley to bring to the Cuban insurgent leader Calixco Garcia y Ignigues. Rowan was not told the contents of the letter, where Garcia was located, how to get to Cuba, and where to trek into the mountains to find the Cuban. Rowan was simply told to bring a message to Garcia. The young officer accomplished his mission, and the rest is history. The insurgency was won. and Cuba gained independence from Spanish rule.

Hubbard concludes his story by writing:

"Civilization is one long anxious search for just such individuals. Anything such a man asks shall be granted. He is wanted in every city, town, and village—in every office, shop, store, and factory. The world cries out for such: he is needed and needed badly—the man who can *Carry the Message to Garcia*."

The definition of initiative is the ability to assess and initiate things independently. This is one of the most important soft skills a person can possess, and it is the hardest to teach and learn. Initiative is difficult to instruct because it requires a leader to give an employee tasks where the person in charge is willing to accept failure. It's a rare leader who has that kind of courage, especially when winning and losing (whether money, a big business deal, or lives in combat) is at stake.

Trust (up and down the org chart) is the foundation in building initiative. The leader has to trust the person carrying out the mission to get it done, and the man or woman doing the work has to trust that the leader will not fire them if they fail.

When I was a company commander in 1993, we were conducting combat training exercise with live ammunition. David H. Petraeus was my battalion commander. One afternoon, Petraeus was there to observe, so I escorted him and a brigadier general who was our assistant division commander. The three of us followed some distance behind one squad as they tossed a hand grenade into a bunker, cleared it with fire, then moved to another bunker to repeat the drill.

I watched as the last soldier cleared the bunker. He was trotting back to his squad for the next assault, rifle in hand, when he tripped and fell. When he hit the ground, rifle still in hand, it went off.

A moment later Petraeus grabbed at his chest, stumbled forward, went down to his knees, and fell cold onto his back.

The general took a quick step over, glanced at the wound, and said, "You're gonna be all right, Dave."

"Fred, he's been shot," the general said, stepping over Petraeus. "I'm going to my helicopter to call in a medevac."

I ran over to Petraeus and unbuttoned the blouse of his uniform. As I did, a small trickle of blood ran from the entry wound, a tiny hole in the front of his chest. I rolled him to his side to look for an exit wound and he groaned; there was a gaping hole in his back as big around as a coffee mug. He had a sucking chest wound; when I laid him flat again, he started spitting up blood and pink tissue.

Two of my soldiers, Specialists Smith and Curtain, rushed over and shoved me aside. "We got this, sir," Curtain said. They sealed the wound with bandages and plastic bags so Petraeus could breathe, then tied off the bags with knots. He was placed on a stretcher about the time the medevac arrived, and he was taken by the helicopter to Vanderbilt University Medical Center for surgery.

After the medevac departed, the general called me and the officer in charge of the exercise over to the helicopter that would take the him back to the division headquarters where he would have to give a report on the incident and check on Petraeus' status.

The general had been my brigade commander at Fort Drum, New York when I was a lieutenant. He would later go on to earn four stars and serve as the Vice Chief of Staff of the Army. He once said, "It's not good training unless someone gets shot every now and then." The irony was not lost on me as I stood at attention in front of him and awaited his guidance.

The general was about 6' 5" and towered over both of us. He had commanded a company in Vietnam and received the Silver Star. His piercing blue eyes looked straight into your soul in a mesmeric way that demanded your immediate respect and obedience. I had, on more than one occasion, stood in the way of that gaze at Fort Drum and was just as possessed by it on the range at Fort Campbell that day as I was as a young lieutenant.

The general said to us, "I want you to do an after-action review with the soldiers and leaders about what happened. Have the squad go through a couple blank fire iterations, and then I want them to do the exercise again with live ammunition." The officer-in-charge of the range was dumbfounded. He had served in a mechanized unit in Germany prior to coming to the 101st, and this was unheard of in most Army organizations. He thought the general had called us over to relieve of us of our commands. My fellow officer incredulously asked him if he meant the soldier that shot Petraeus as well. The general looked at him with his blue eyes and said, "Especially that soldier." He then got on his helicopter and flew away.

Petraeus recovered from his wound and returned to the battalion less than a month later. Evidently, his doctor told him that he was not ready to leave, so Petraeus did 50 pushups and said it was time he got back to the battalion. He called me into his office before physical training the morning he returned. I reported to him, and he told me to come in and take a seat. I thought for sure that I was going be fired from my job. That is what normally happens with serious incidents such as had occurred on the range.

Petraeus put down some papers he was reviewing. He looked at me for a moment and said, "You know, Fred, there is a rumor going around the battalion. The rumor is that the soldier was actually aiming at you and hit me." I thought he was serious for a second and then he laughed, "That would speak volumes for both your bad leadership and your company's poor marksmanship, wouldn't it? Loosen up, Fred. That's a joke." He laughed again and told me, "Mistakes happen. But remember: live up to your potential and pass on a second chance. Now, get back to work, company commander."

There are not too many leaders who would have a subordinate get them shot and let it go without severe punishment—it's unheard of. However, Petraeus not only allowed me to keep my job, he gave me an outstanding evaluation at the end of my tour, which contributed to my early promotion to the rank of Major. He trusted that I learned from my mistake and it wouldn't happen again. That instilled a special kind of initiative in me because I knew I could take reasonable risk without fearing Petraeus would crush me.

The power of a second chance coupled with good mentorship can mobilize incredible potential (and initiative) in our employees.

Blood, Sweat, Tyranny, and Training

The Open Knob was a superior position for the Union forces under the command of Brigadier General William Terrill. They had good visibility and great fields of fire to engage Maney's brigade, who had to negotiate the fence and then fight up a steep incline. The forces were also equally matched in numbers. This was an advantage for the Federals because conventional battlefield calculus requires a ratio of 3:1 in favor of the attacking force over an enemy that was in the defense. It would appear that the odds were in Terrill's favor.

However, there were a couple significant drawbacks working against Terrill's brigade, which was comprised of the 80th and 123rd Illinois and the 105th Ohio.

Many of the troops in these organizations arrived to Louisville only five days since their induction and first muster. Most of the soldiers had never fired their weapon, and they had almost no tactical training. Not long after their arrival, they began the long march under horrid conditions to Perryville. To make matters worse, Brigadier General Jackson did not allow his soldiers to eat breakfast and restricted their water consumption before the battle.

When they arrived to the battlefield, these green, poorly trained, tired, and hungry soldiers were placed on the Union right flank, one of the most important and decisive spots in the Federals' defense. If

Terrill's brigade lost the flank, it would be much easier for the Confederates to roll up the rest of the formation and defeat the Army of the Ohio.

The night before the battle Jackson, Terrill and another brigade commander, Colonel Charles Webster, talked about the prospects of all three leaders being killed the same day. Jackson said, "It was nearly mathematically impossible for all of them to die during the fight."

Spoiler alert! He was wrong.

Jackson was killed on the Open Knob during the fight, and the soldiers under his command left the general's body on the battlefield. This was an unheard-of show of disrespect and demonstrated how much the general was despised. However, Jackson was not the only leader hated by the troops.

Brigadier General Terrill fought with distinction as a captain and artillery battery commander at the battles of Shiloh and Richmond (Kentucky) just a few months previously. Ironically, he faced Brigadier General Maney at Shiloh and repelled the Confederate attack and was recognized for his gallantry. Not long afterwards, Terrill was promoted several ranks to brigadier general and put in command of an infantry brigade. He was disliked by his soldiers and seen as an extension of Brigadier General Jackson's tyranny. Some swore they would take his life because of his poor leadership.

In contrast to the soldiers in Terrill's brigade, the men at the bottom of the hill preparing to charge were seasoned veterans, and Brigadier General George Maney was leading them. He hoped to have his revenge for Shiloh.

Maney's attack came in like waves that ebbed and flowed. With every bit of ground that was gained, some would be lost as Parson's battery and musket fire rained lead against them. However, they continued to make steady progress until it was almost certain they would take the hill.

Terrill became fixated on his artillery, the thing he knew best. At times he personally directed the cannon fire even though it was Captain Parson's job and he was very good at it. Terrill lost focus on his primary responsibility of leading his brigade and maneuvering the infantry. In a moment of desperation, Terrill ordered the 123d Illinois to make a bayonet charge against Maney's brigade. To assume the correct alignment for the assault, the soldiers were given an order to come on a line of twos with the intent that the tallest men would be in the rear and the smallest in the front. They had no training on this particular movement and got it backwards. Furthermore, many of the soldiers didn't even know how to attach their bayonets.

Regardless, they charged. And they were slaughtered.

The 123rd Illinois lost 25 percent of their men. Albion Tourgee of the 105th Ohio wrote of the bayonet charge, "… that it was only justifiable to gain time to withdraw the battery or for the arrival of expected reinforcements. As a way to attempt to take the enemy's position or repel their attack, it was simple madness … the fear of losing his battery blinded him to all other considerations."

Terrill broke under combat stress. Not long after the failed bayonet charge he was hit by shrapnel and later died. Colonel Charles Webster would be killed not long afterwards.

As a result of Jackson and Terrill's horrible leadership, the line broke in 30 minutes. With Webster dead, there was no one in charge of the Union formation. The remaining soldiers from Terrill's brigade panicked and went into full retreat.

Brigadier General Lovell Rousseau commanded the 3rd Division, which was to the right of Jackson. As soldiers from Terrill's brigade fled, Rousseau galloped forward on his horse and started striking men with the flat of his sword until he broke it. He then put his hat on the end of his broken sword and rallied the men saying, "We'll whip them yet."

Had Rousseau not intervened, the fleeing troops might not have stopped running until they were completely off the battlefield. Moreover, most of the soldiers Rousseau rallied would be repositioned at a very decisive location on the battlefield that would result in a positive outcome later in the fight.

Soft Skill Lessons

➢ A leader should know the strengths and weaknesses of his or her organization. The soldiers in Terrill's brigade were not experienced or skilled enough to be placed in the most important place on the Union line. Where are the weak flanks in your organization and how do you bolster them?

➢ When Terrill became stressed he reverted back to his comfort zone and the skill set he knew best. What measures can leaders take to prevent this from happening?

➢ Terrill was promoted five ranks and given command of an organization he was ill prepared to lead. How did his lack of experience affect his decision-making? How could Brigadier General Jackson have better prepared his subordinate commander?

➢ All the key senior leaders in Jackson's Division were killed. No one was left in charge to lead the battle, and it took Brigadier General Rousseau, a commander from an entirely different organization, to insert himself and stop the retreat. Have you prepared subordinate leaders to step up when key personnel are unavailable?

Leaders Worth Following

My initial tour of duty in the military was with the newly created 10th Mountain Division (Light). That's where I served with Carlin

Brumback. At the time, the Army saw the need to establish light infantry divisions because we expected to have to fight in locations (like South America) where mechanized forces could not be effectively employed. One of the criteria to serve in the 10th Mountain Division was that officers had to be Ranger qualified. Less than 50 percent of the people who attended Ranger training graduated, so the people who were assigned there were a select group of leaders.

The division was comprised of the most remarkable group of senior officers assembled in one place in the Army. Most all of them were hand selected to help form the division, and nearly all of them served in Vietnam. It was a tremendous place to grow up as a junior officer. I loved the leaders with whom I served. I assumed the entire military had such inspirational men and women. I departed the 10th Mountain Division thinking I would never leave the Army.

My next assignment was in the 101st Airborne Division (Air Assault). As is the custom, newly arrived officers report to the battalion personnel officer or S1 for in-processing. I learned that I would be assuming his position. The S1 gave me a page listing all of his former duties, which were now my duties. They included keeping the commander's refrigerator filled with Fresca, seeing that the commander's vehicle was always clean, writing thank-you letters, and picking up the commander's laundry at the cleaners. It was a long list if things that had nothing to do with preparing for war.

When I finally met the commander, I felt a vicious coldness inside, the kind of feeling you'd have if you were caught out in the December rain with no jacket. The sharp chill would fade when I wasn't around him, but it came back every time I heard his voice. There could not have been anyone more opposite of the leaders I served with at Fort Drum.

He was a very small man with delicate features. He was perfectly kept, with a starched uniform and fingernails I swore had to be manicured. His hair was much longer than I'd ever seen on an officer; I had a short high-and-tight. He was much too young to have been in Vietnam and had never served in combat. He never talked about war, his vocation; instead he focused on social engagements, on finding opportunities to meet with the commanding general and other senior officers.

It wasn't long into the job before I realized nothing would ever compare to Fort Drum and the people with whom I'd served there.

One day I went to the garrison lawyer, who helped me draft a letter of resignation. I signed the letter and kept it in my office drawer, waiting until the right moment. I was done. I had to get out before it went too far and I did something stupid, like beating the crap out of my boss. I finally submitted the letter to my battalion and brigade commanders, and they endorsed it. But before it was sent forward to the division headquarters for final processing, Iraq invaded Kuwait and we were alerted to deploy. I told the commanders that I changed my mind and really didn't want to resign, so they returned the letter to me. I tore it up and went to the First Gulf War with the Screaming Eagles of the 101st.

Fortunately, I saw the commander only rarely in Saudi Arabia, where we were located prior to the attack into Iraq. Not long after we arrived in country, he contracted what we called the NVDs—nausea, vomiting, and diarrhea. The NVDs were common, but most soldiers recovered in a couple days; the commander had it for about three months. He spent the majority of Desert Shield in the aid tent hooked up to IVs.

One day, the battalion command sergeant major, or CSM, and I were driving around, checking on the troops, when we saw the commander's driver tip-toeing to the laundry. He was holding a set of desert camouflage fatigues still wet with shit, his fingertips and arms extended fully away from his nose. We pulled up beside the driver and the CSM asked him, "What in the hell are you doing, Sergeant?"

The young sergeant turned his head to the CSM, keeping his nose up and away from the uniform, and said, "The commander shit himself again, so he told me to wash it."

The CSM shoved the shifter into park, sprang out of the car, and snatched the uniform from the sergeant. With the same hand he threw open the tent's door, stepped inside, and marched over to the commander, who lay groaning on a gurney. He threw the soiled fatigues at the commander and said, "Sir, the next time you shit yourself, you call me to wash your uniform. But *never* order that soldier to do it again."

After a month-long air campaign against Iraq, the ground war was ready to begin. The day before the attack, I noticed the commander wasn't on the manifest to accompany the main attack force by helicopter. I asked another captain—a staff officer who'd been in the battalion much longer than me— if there was some mistake. He shook his head in disgust.

"I just heard this from a guy at division headquarters—so it may or may not be true—but, evidently, our fearless leader had a premonition that he'd die," the captain said. "So he's made the courageous decision to drive up with the logistics convoy and, um, *follow* us into battle. You know, to ensure our much-needed supplies arrive on time."

On February 24, 1991, I was 29 years old—and I walked out onto the Saudi Arabian desert to a stretch of attack helicopters as far as the eye could see. I rode a Black Hawk helicopter 155 miles into Iraq, across the Euphrates River valley where the most ancient civilizations rose and fell.

Our commander wasn't there to see it though. He didn't arrive to our location on the battlefield until the war had almost ended. That commander had a lasting effect on me. I swore I would never be like him. That was his legacy. Sometimes you learn how to be a leader by serving under a person who isn't one.

Thankfully, David Petraeus assumed command of the battalion after the war. As a result of his leadership and inspiration I would go on to serve another 21 years.

While my battalion commander that preceded Petraeus was a horrible leader, the 500,000 U.S. service members that participated in Desert Shield and Storm were fortunate to have two tremendous officers in charge at the highest level of our organization—General Norman Schwarzkopf and General Colin Powell.

The ground attack during Desert Storm lasted 100 hours.

There were critics who said Desert Storm wasn't even a war. Someone actually said to me, "We only lost 292 soldiers, 147 of them in combat-related deaths. That's not a war. Not enough people died." Others commented that Iraq had a second-rate army and they should have been easily defeated. And still more shrugged and remarked, "It just wasn't long enough to really be a war."

In every case, these words came from people who were not there alongside us in the sand. They didn't know the danger or understand our fear. Moreover, they did not consider that while combat lasted four days, we had been in Saudi Arabia five months preparing and training for the invasion.

There were politicians who demurred that we should attack immediately. Thankfully, calmer, more experienced heads prevailed and we waited until we were ready.

As we trained and prepared for the attack into Iraq, Schwarzkopf would tell us, "The more you sweat in peace, the less you bleed in war."

Another contributing factor to our victory during Desert Storm is that we conducted the war using the Powell Doctrine. First, we set the conditions for success, then we directed overwhelming strength at the enemy's weakness and finally we had a sound exit strategy after the conflict was won.

Are you a Schwarzkopf or the guy with NVDs? How well have the Union and Confederate leaders applied the Powell Doctrine so far in the Battle of Perryville? Does the Powell Doctrine apply to your business?

My Kingdom for a Horse

Maney now controlled the Open Knob and the cannons that were left abandoned there. The artillery was a prized possession. Normally, the artillery would be moved to an alternate location when a position was in threat of being overrun. However, the Rebels employed a tactic that would impede the displacement of the cannons.

There were eight cannons on the Open Knob. It takes six horses to move a single cannon and the limber, which has another set of wheels and helps carry the artillery piece. It takes an additional six horses to move the caisson, which carries the ammunition. That's 96 horses. The horses had to be put in a place of relative safety and a location that could accommodate that large number. As a result, they were positioned in a field behind the Open Knob.

The Confederates placed their own artillery battery so it could range the Open Knob and the field where the horses were located. They would alternate firing on the hill against the soldiers there and the field where the horses waited. The horses were killed, and the Union cannons could not be moved. Only one of the artillery pieces was moved off the Open Knob.

Once Maney took the Open Knob, he turned the artillery on the retreating soldiers of Terrill's brigade.

Soft Skill Lessons

➤ The Confederates employed an *out the box* method by firing upon the horses that moved the cannons. In the military this is called an "asymmetric attack."

- ➢ What are some of the ways you can accomplish a task asymmetrically in the workplace?
- ➢ Are there ways to get at your mission and vision without going directly at the competition?

Thinking Outside the Box

Creativity is often the product of necessity. However, it is also the result of linking experiences together to help solve problems. Steve Jobs said:

"Creativity is just connecting things. When you ask creative people how they did something, they feel a little guilty because they didn't really do it, they just saw something. It seemed obvious to them after a while. That's because they were able to connect experiences they've had and synthesize new things."

Maney's tactic of firing on the horses to prevent the displacement of the Union artillery was created out of the necessity to render one of the greatest killers on the battlefield ineffective. The cannons were killing his people. However, his experience and understanding of how the big guns were maneuvered shaped a way, in his mind, to defeat them without actually destroying the equipment and hardware, which could be used by his forces against the enemy later in the fight.

This is called an *asymmetric* approach to problem solving. It is not always the direct method that achieves the greatest results.

General Petraeus used an asymmetric tactic in the Second Gulf War in 2004. Not long after the invasion, he recognized the conflict had evolved into a counterinsurgency. The U.S. was not fighting a conventional enemy; rather, the struggle was against paramilitary and terrorist forces that directed their attacks against both our army and the civilian population.

Petraeus was a student of history and understood that the citizens of Iraq must be made to feel safe and secure. They must also have a sense of hope that their situation was getting better and that it was the insurgents, not the U.S., that undermined their prosperity. One of the ways to demonstrate an increase of wellbeing for the populace was to improve the infrastructure and get people back to work. This could only be accomplished by directing financial resources toward the problem. Petraeus made a bold claim by saying:

"Money is my most important ammunition in this war."

This was a completely *out of the box* way of thinking about how to defeat the enemy. Petraeus experienced great success while he was in command of the 101st Airborne Division (Air Assault) and responsible for Mosul, the second largest city in Iraq. This idea of money as ammunition was later incorporated into military doctrine and still used today.

So, That's What Fear Looks Like

Private Sam Watkins served in the 1st Tennessee and fought at Perryville and in other major battles, including Shiloh. He was one of only seven men in his company that survived the Civil War. Watkins said of the Battle of Perryville:

"We were soon in a hand-to-hand fight—every man for himself—using the butts of our guns and bayonets. One side would waver and fall back a few yards, and would rally, when the other side would fall back … and yet the battle raged. Such obstinate fighting I never had seen before or since. The guns were discharged so rapidly that it seemed the earth itself was in a volcanic uproar. The iron storm passed through our ranks, mangling and tearing men to pieces. The very air seemed full of stifling smoke and fire, which seemed the very pit of hell, peopled by contending demons."

It is impossible for me to imagine a person not being afraid in the sorts of conditions described by Watkins. Nelson Mandela said, "I learned that courage was not the absence of fear, but the triumph over it. The brave man is not he who does not feel afraid, but he who conquers that fear."

It is not only fear we have to control in war or the workplace but also other emotions like anger, frustration, and anxiety. We must have the situational awareness to know that they exist in us, what the triggers are and how to mitigate their presence in our demeanor.

Soft Skill Lessons:

➢ How do you recognize if you, personally, need work controlling emotional response?

➢ What are the steps you take to address and fix the problem if it exists?

➢ How do you counsel your employees who struggle with controlling emotional response? What steps do you take to help them?

Emotional Response Control

In 2009, I was a marketing brigade commander, responsible for around 300 people who told the Army story across the country to help with the recruiting mission. The Golden Knights, the Army's premier freefall parachute team, was an organization in the brigade. The day before I took command I had an opportunity to do a tandem jump. A tandem is when you are attached snugly to an experienced skydiver and you jump together from about 2.5 miles above the earth.

I had done about 36 static-line parachute jumps in my career from 1,000 to 1,500 feet. Other than situational awareness and some body position requirements upon exiting and landing, basic parachuting is fairly simple. However, it would be considered a hard skill because of those technical aptitudes that must be mastered.

There is a song we sang (a cadence, it's called) while we did our morning runs in Airborne School that summarizes the process:

Stand up, hook up, shuffle to the door
Jump right out and count to four
If your main (parachute) doesn't open wide
You have a reserve (parachute) by your side
If that one should fail you too
Look out below you're coming through.

Even though I hadn't jumped in almost 15 years, I felt confident that the tandem job would be a fun adventure. After all I would be to a world-class skydiver who was doing all the work. We suited up, put on our parachutes, and boarded the aircraft. As we climbed in altitude, I watched the buildings and people get smaller and smaller. It started to occur to me that we were pretty far up. I would never admit it to anyone, but I was starting to get a bad case of the butterflies.

Then it was time. My tandem skydiver attached the device that bound us together. The door opened, the wind and noise rushed in, and we scuffled to the exit. A Golden Knight was assigned as the videographer. He had a camera attached to his helmet and filmed the entire event from actions within the aircraft through our landing. As I stood in the door, he was holding on to the frame of the plane with one hand and hanging outside of it giving me the thumps up and trying to make me laugh. I put on my best fake smile. I was ready to get this thing done.

We rocked back and forth and counted to three. On three we were out the door. The freefall lasted about one minute, then the Golden Knight pulled the ripcord, the parachute opened, and we glided through the air for another five minutes or so before landing. It was a pretty cool experience, but I was happy it was over.

When it's all done, the Golden Knights give you the video of the event. I was eager to take it home to show my family how brave I was to jump out of a perfectly good airplane. After dinner, I put the video in the television, and we scooted close to the screen so my 12-year-old daughter, Madelyn, could watch her Airborne, Ranger, combat infantryman dad be a badass.

However, as I watched the recording and observed my face and body language, I noticed nervous fidgeting in the aircraft. I saw my eyes grow big and dart back and forth. My bottom lip even quivered a bit. My beautiful brown-eyed daughter then tugged gently at my shirtsleeve. I turned to look at her anticipating a compliment, and she said brightly,

"So, Daddy, that's what fear looks like."

Controlling emotional response is a very important soft skill. Failure to restrain anger, frustration, and overt disapproval can have an adverse impact on workplace effectiveness. Imagine a boss showing uncontrolled dread in front of their employees as the company faces a big layoff or a business deal has gone bad. Fear spreads like wildfire in an organization, and the panic can ruin morale, productivity, and faith in the leader.

For those of us who are high strung (like myself), controlling emotional response requires a higher degree of self-discipline and training than those who are less anxious. Of all my soft skill shortfalls, this one demands my greatest attention. I have been in therapy for some time to address my PTSD, so I have a trained psychologist who provides the cognitive tools to help me. I also practice yoga and mindfulness. Nonetheless, it is hard work, and every leader must master it.

As it pertains to fear specifically, the military's approach to addressing the problem is through training and repetition. The more confidence a soldier has in their hard skill proficiency (employing their weapon, rendering first aid, movement techniques, etc.), the less they are afraid when it is time to use them in combat. As an officer, we had classes and staff rides (like the Perryville Battlefield Leadership Experience) on how to confront fear. We were also put in situations that produced fear, like climbing a 30-foot rope and cargo net at least weekly. Finally, the most effective way to reduce fear is unit cohesion. People who are confident in their leaders and the men and women they work alongside are less afraid in challenging times.

Colonel Terrill is a perfect example of someone who had not learned to control emotional response —you see the result.

Ich Spreche Kein Deutsch

Colonel John Starkweather's brigade was positioned on a hilltop almost 1,000 yards directly to the rear of Terrill. Brigadier General Lovell Roussaeu was the division commander and Starkweather's boss. The 21st Wisconsin was a part of Starkweather's brigade and was comprised of a significant number of former Prussian soldiers who had fought in European wars prior to coming to the United States. Many of the Prussians were strict abolitionists.

Before the start of the battle, two slaves come into the 21st Wisconsin camp followed by several slave catchers. Men of the 21st Wisconsin stopped the slave catchers and wanted to lynch them. A messenger was sent to inform Brigadier General Rousseau, who sent back a note ordering them to let the slave catchers go. The 21st refused. Rousseau was again notified, and this time he rode out to the camp to take care of the problem himself. Rousseau ordered the men of the 21st to stack their arms. He then directed soldiers from another unit, the 79th Pennsylvania, to load their muskets and aim them at the 21st. Rousseau then said, "21st will you now obey my orders?" A single soldier answered, "Yes, General, if consistent with our duty and our conscience, but no slave catching." Rousseau demanded to know who made that comment. Five men stepped forward.

The situation was resolved, but there was tension in the ranks. One of the reasons the Prussians joined the Union Army was to fight and end slavery. The problem, however, was that the legal provision of the Emancipation Proclamation would not go into effect until January 1, 1863. Slavery was still allowed, though Kentucky was currently exempt from the Emancipation Proclamation. Nonetheless, the Union was still trying to appease the native Kentuckians so they would not align with the Confederacy.

Soft Skill Lessons

➢ How well do you manage differing viewpoints and cultures within your organization? Could have Rousseau handled the situation better? How?

➢ What role did empathy and an understanding of cultural diversity play in this particular event?

Empathy

Brigadier General Rousseau nearly shot men because of differing opinions on what to do with the runaway slaves. In Rousseau's mind he was upholding the law and maintaining reasonable relations with the local population. The men of the 21st Wisconsin believed the very reason they were risking their lives (to end slavery) was being undermined. Rousseau's severe response to the former Prussian soldiers objection may have also been a matter of discipline because the commander's orders were disobeyed. Rousseau would later direct that the 21st Wisconsin be positioned in a cornfield in proximity to Terrill's brigade where the action would be the hottest. Some have asserted this was a punishment for the 21st's show of disrespect. Regardless, Rousseau seemed to lack empathy and an understanding of the cultural differences with the Prussian immigrants.

In August of 2011, I had been in Kabul, Afghanistan for a little over a week. It was during Ramadan and very hot. I was walking with a buddy to the Ministry of Defense where I worked. As we approached the gate, an Afghan soldier was standing guard. For some unknown reason my friend removed a bottle of Coke out of his pocket, unscrewed the top, and took a drink. I was aghast. Muslims do not eat or drink from sunrise to sunset during the Muslim holy month. This was an insult, and I hoped that the guard did not notice. He did and watched us with disgust as we neared the gate.

At the entrance, I placed my hand over my heart, as it the custom, and said, "Sa-laam Alaykum," which means "Peace be with you." I waited for the reply, which should have been "Walaykum Assalaam," offering peace to me in return. The guard didn't say a word. He just nodded his head as if to say resentfully, "You may pass."

I made a commitment that day to make amends with the guard and ultimately gain his respect. I started learning Dari, which is the official language of Afghanistan.

One morning at the gate I rendered the traditional greeting of "Salaam Alaykum" and followed it immediately with "Sobh bekheir, chetoori," which means "Good morning, how are you?" The guard looked at me with complete surprise. After a prolonged silence he answered in decent English, "I'm good, Johnson. Thanks." I asked how he knew my name, and he pointed to the badge on my jacket. "Kind of obvious," he replied and then said, "Walaykum Assalaam. My name is Heytabullah, and by the way, Johnson, your Dari sucks."

Over the next several months Heytabullah took it upon himself to become my Dari teacher. We would spend lunch together and he would teach me phrases in Dari and other aspects of the Afghan culture. One of the things I noticed was that Afghans would greet one another with kisses on both cheeks. Heytabullah and I never kissed. I wanted a kiss badly.

One evening when I was leaving work, Heytabullah told me not to come to the Ministry of Defense the next day. I asked him why and he wouldn't say. I didn't think anything else about it. However, the next morning as I was about to depart my living area, explosions and gunfire came from the Ministry. We were locked down and couldn't leave for several days. Several people were killed in the attack. When we were finally released, I ran to make sure Heytabullah was okay. I was relieved to see him standing guard at the gate. We never talked about the event again or how he knew an attack was going to take place.

I spent nine months in Afghanistan. The day before I left I went to say goodbye to Heytabullah. As I approached him, Heytabullah stretched his neck and looked down the road. He shouted, "Johnson! Cheekgo paz, lappo jap"—Dari slang for "What's happening?" We exchanged our usual greetings. Heytabullah took my hand and held it loosely. We spoke for a while, and then I had to go. Heytabullah took me by the shoulders and pulled me into him. He pressed his cheek against mine and kissed me. I did the same to him. We released one another. Then he said, "Let me walk you to the doorway." We held hands like schoolchildren while we walked past the other guards to the gate. It was my proudest moment in Afghanistan. I wish someone had taken a picture—but no one would have thought to, because in Afghanistan that's just what friends do.

My experience in Afghanistan was unlike any of the other wars I had participated. I was an advisor to the Chief of Staff of the Afghan Army. I was never in direct combat. The battle I faced wasn't against an enemy per se. Rather, it was a contest to build the trust and confidence of my Afghan counterparts.

While young men and women were fighting and dying in the mountains and villages of Afghanistan, I was given a different hill to charge. Ironically in this war my success or failure, and even my safety, was not dependent on my abilities as a warrior. It was not an M4 or 9mm that protected me and enabled the accomplishment of my mission. It was empathy.

Caught in the Cornfield

After the Confederates took the Open Knob, they pressed the fight towards Colonel John Starkweather's brigade on the next ridge to the Rebels' immediate front. There was a cornfield between the two opposing forces. The stalks were dense and at least the height of a man. The 21st Wisconsin, which was positioned in the cornfield, had a lot of raw recruits who had not seen action before, and there were the Prussians who did have combat experience. The fear of the untested troops was intensified because they couldn't see what was happening on the Open Knob. However, they knew the fighting was very severe because they could hear the musket and cannon fire along with the screams of wounded and dying men.

The situation worsened when soldiers from Terrill's brigade panicked and began to flee. The terrified troops' route of retreat was straight through the cornfield, and Maney's brigade followed them in pursuit. Both Union and Confederates became mingled within the cornfield in close hand-to-hand combat.

As Maney's brigade continued their attack, their next objective was to take Starkweather's Hill. Colonel Starkweather was faced with a dilemma. He could wait until the Confederates cleared the cornfield and engage them, but at that point Maney would be a mere 200 yards from the top of the ridge where the Federals were positioned. Or he could fire his cannons and muskets into the cornfield and attempt to slow the assault there, the problem being that friendly forces, many of them his men, were in the cornfield intermixed with the enemy.

Starkweather chose to shoot into the cornfield. Hundreds of his men along with many of the attackers were killed or wounded. Maney's assault was stalled, momentarily.

Soft Skill Lessons

➢ Problem-solving is an important soft skill. Many times solutions to problems require making difficult decisions.

➢ Are there times in the workplace when you have to make sacrifices for the greater good?

➢ What factors do you weigh when choosing between achieving a business objective and your employee's wellbeing?

Risk Management

There is a saying in the military that goes "Mission first, people always." In my combat experience nearly every time we went on patrol there was a chance we would get in a fight with the enemy. This meant people could get killed or wounded. Fortunately, I never had to make a decision like Starkweather. Nevertheless, I gave orders that put young men and women under my command routinely in harm's way. That is the nature of war.

One of the leaders who had a great influence on me as a young officer was Major General Bill Carpenter. Carpenter commanded the 10th Mountain Division, where I started my Army career. We called him "Napalm Bill" Carpenter because he received the Distinguished Service Cross (an award for gallantry just below the Medal of Honor) as a captain in Vietnam. Enemy forces were about to overrun his company, and it looked like his entire unit would be annihilated. He radioed the air traffic controller and said, "We're overrun; they're right in among us. I need an air strike on my position." Airplanes dropped napalm right on top of Carpenter and his soldiers. Legend has it when asked how he could kill some of his own men, he replied, "So the majority could live."

When I was in the 10th Mountain, we were on a field training exercise and I failed a mission miserably. I didn't aggressively pursue the enemy, and they called indirect fire on us. My platoon was wiped out with simulated casualties. Major General Carpenter was there to observe the event. Afterwards, he gripped the back of my neck with his huge thick hand and said to me, "Son, you have to kill the people who are killing you."

I never forgot his advice.

When I was in Mosul, Iraq in 2006 I was on patrol with a platoon from the 18th Engineer Company looking for improvised explosive devices (IEDs). I was in the third vehicle of the convoy and the lead truck stopped below an underpass. A call came over the radio from the lieutenant who was leading the mission. He reported, "I have good news, and I have bad news." There was a moment of silence. Then he continued, "The good news is that I found an IED. The bad news is that it is directly over my head."

Normally, the enemy had observers watching the IEDs and detonated them when our vehicles were in the kill zone. This was a nasty situation.

The 18th Engineer Company, by far, had the most engagements with the enemy of any unit in my battalion during the deployment. They were comprised of the most courageous and competent group of officers and NCOs with whom I have served. This particular platoon had been in similar situations and knew what they were up against.

I had a couple of choices. We could back out from the underpass and call in an Explosive Ordnance Detachment (EOD) to disarm the bomb. Or, the lieutenant's team of engineers could do it. They were trained for that mission after all.

I made the call for the lieutenant to defuse the IED. I felt there was too much risk leaving it there and waiting for EOD because heavy civilian traffic moved on that road. Often, the enemy doesn't discriminate who they blow up, even if it was their own people. One of our key tasks was to protect the Iraqi people. Moreover, if the lieutenant did his work quickly he could get the job done before it exploded.

We then quickly deployed the remaining vehicles to secure the area and attempt to flush out the enemy observer or at least make them leave without detonating the explosive device. Fortunately, that worked, and the IED was disabled without incident.

Mission first, people always—that is the burden great leaders must shoulder, always keeping the two in mind.

The High Water Mark of the Confederacy in the West

Starkweather's brigade represented the last hope of securing the Union left flank and stopping the Confederates from rolling up the remainder of the Army of the Ohio. A portion of Brigadier General Alexander Stewart's brigade had now joined Maney in the attack, making an even more formidable force to defend against.

There were 13 cannons on Starkweather's Hill. However, as Maney and Stewart pressed the fight against the Federal position, the men manning the artillery retreated and left the cannons unoccupied. Fortunately, Sergeant John Otto and a soldier named Loewenweld stepped into the breach. Both were from the 21st Wisconsin and had previously fought in the Prussian Army. They manned the cannons and fired into the Rebels, stalling their attack. When Starkweather asked, "Who runs this concern?" Otto answered, "We are running this business on shares, but here Loewenweld serves as a captain without commission." Starkweather replied, "Well, give them hell."

They gave them hell, but not enough of it. The combined forces of Maney and Stewart could not be stopped. Starkweather was driven off the hill and forced to withdraw to another ridgeline further to their rear.

During Starkweather's rearward movement, the brigade's color sergeant was killed. The color sergeant was a very important assignment during the Civil War. He carried the flag with the unit insignia. In the heat of combat, with the noise and smoke, the colors represented one of the most important communication devices on the battlefield. They provided the soldiers a visible object to focus on during the attack. When the colors were lost, troops may not know where to go or what to do. When the color sergeant was killed, Sergeant John S. Durham picked of the colors and helped lead a counterattack, which allowed the successful repositioning of Starkweather's brigade behind a stone wall on dominating ridgeline.

Sergeant Durham received the Medal of Honor for his actions.

The combination of the exhaustion of Maney and Stewart's soldiers, who were running short on ammunition and water, the steepness of the incline of the ridgeline, and the stonewall that offered the Union protection resulted in the culmination of the Rebel attack.

Colonel Starkweather saved the Army of the Ohio.

In Kenneth Noe's book, *This Grand Havoc of Battle*, he wrote, "The high water mark of the Confederacy in the western theater, no less important than the 'Angle' at Gettysburg had been reached. The Union Army, as it had at Gettysburg, held."

Soft Skill Lessons

➢ Who will pick up and carry the colors for your organization like Sergeant Durham? And, who will turn the guns on a problem like Otto and Loewenweld did on Starkweather's Hill? How are you developing that kind of initiative in your employees?

➢ Had it not been Starkweather's never-quit leadership, the Battle of Perryville and the fate of Kentucky could have gone in a much different direction. How do you instill that kind of will in your employees? How do you prepare yourself to be the kind of boss that leads from the front?

➤ How did Generals Bragg, Polk, and Cheatham contribute to Maney's failure in defeating Starkweather?

➤ Starkweather suffered an initial tactical defeat but ultimately contributed to a strategic victory. How do you ensure your employees keep their focus on the primary purpose of your vision and mission?

Adaptability

Innovation strategy specialist Max McKeown said, "Adaptability is about the powerful difference between adapting to cope and adapting to win."

Colonel Starkweather watched Maney's brigade overrun the Open Knob in less than 30 minutes. Then, Stewart's brigade joined the fight and, even after a good effort to hold his position, Starkweather had to withdrawal under heavy pressure from the Rebels. He had to maneuver his brigade to another ridgeline where he got his men behind the stonewall and finally stopped the Confederate attack.

Tenacity and adaptability are closely linked. A good leader must have both a strong will to overcome obstacles and the mental clarity to see opportunities to surmount the challenges.

General Petraeus was unquestionably tenacious. It takes a rare breed of person who can sustain a gunshot wound to the chest and return to work five weeks later (and run with his soldiers). This tenacity complemented his adaptability, which produced remarkable results.

When Petraeus was the commander of the 101st Airborne Division (Air Assault) in Mosul, Iraq, he was required to meet with local Iraqi leaders regularly. Each meeting could require a different approach based on the objectives of the gathering and the personalities of Iraqi attendees. Sometimes he would sit and drink tea for hours on end without ever discussing an agenda item. Other times, he would abruptly storm in and show his dissatisfaction that progress wasn't being made in a timely fashion. These were conscious, well-thought-out tactics and certainly never reactionary.

As I discussed earlier, Petraeus was one of the first leaders to recognize the nature of the war had changed from a conventional battle to a counterinsurgency. Many of his senior leaders, including Defense Secretary Donald Rumsfeld, dismissed the notion entirely. (In fact, Rumsfeld allegedly reprimanded Petraeus.) Moreover, some of his junior leaders failed to respond to the general's new approach to defeating the enemy. Many of them wanted to continue to conduct raids that destroyed Iraqi infrastructure, killed innocents, and angered civilians who would then support the insurgents. Petraeus would say, "You can't kill your way out of an insurgency," and this flew in the face of the traditional American way of war.

Petraeus took a good deal of risk pursuing a course of action that ran in opposition to standard operating procedures, particularly when they were in defiance to his boss. However, risk management is an important component of adaptability. The key thing to remember, though, is the difference between risk and a gamble. If you take a risk and fail, it can be overcome. If you gamble and fail, the result can't be salvaged—it's a catastrophic loss. There is a fine line that separates the two and great leaders can see the tipping point.

CHAPTER 8

The Aftermath of the Battle of Perryville

"I was in every battle, skirmish, and march that was made by the First Tennessee Regiment during the war, and I do not remember of a harder contest and more evenly fought battle than that of Perryville. If it had been two men wrestling, it would have been called a 'dog fall.' Both sides claim victory—both whipped."— *Private Sam Watkins*

Arguably, the Army of the Mississippi could claim a victory over the Army of the Ohio at the Battle of Perryville. The Union had 4,276 casualties with 894 killed, 2,911 wounded, and 471 captured or missing compared to 3,401 Confederate casualties, which included 532 killed, 2,641 wounded, and 228 captured or missing.

The Rebels engaged just a portion of Buell's Army at Perryville. Coming into battle the Army of the Ohio had three corps comprised of approximately 55,200 men. Nonetheless, only 22,000 soldiers, mostly from Major General McDowell McCook's I Corps, got into the fight. Buell made a huge tactical error by not massing his forces. There is good reason to believe the acoustic shadow played a significant role in the commander's poor decision-making.

Bragg, on the other hand, had 16,500 soldiers in his army, most all of whom were deployed in the battle. However, Major General Kirby-Smith had about 2,000 men, but he never got to Perryville. Part of the reason for this was the loose command relationship between the two leaders.

If Buell had maneuvered all his available troops, the outcome of the battle would most likely have been much different. Instead, it was nearly an even match. Regardless, at the end of the day on October 8, Bragg learned that the other 28,000 Union soldiers from II and III Corps were in striking distance of Perryville. To continue the battle the next day would most assuredly result in a total defeat of his army. At 9 p.m. Bragg ordered his subordinate commanders to begin a withdrawal by midnight. They were forced to leave 900 wounded men behind.

Bragg and Smith eventually consolidated their forces. However, it became clear that Kentucky was not going to provide the number of soldiers that had been promised and that the state lack the logistical support to sustain the Confederate Army. Rebel and Union forces had several small skirmishes, but there was never an outright attack. Bragg soon left Kentucky through the Cumberland Gap and eventually made it to Knoxville, Tennessee. Buell made an unenthusiastic pursuit of Bragg, but the Union commander finally went to Nashville instead of continuing southeast to Knoxville.

The Confederates left Kentucky never to return. The Bluegrass State remained securely under Union control for the remainder of the war.

Bragg was called to Richmond, Virginia to explain to Jefferson Davis why the Kentucky campaign failed. He was left in command, but he never regained the trust of his officers or the President of the Confederacy. Buell, on the other hand, was relieved of command (for a second time) because he disobeyed President Lincoln's orders to pursue and destroy Bragg's army in Tennessee. He was never given command again and resigned from service in 1864 before the end of the war.

Civil War historian James M. McPherson called the Battle of Perryville a turning point in the war. He wrote, "The battles at Antietam and Perryville threw back Confederate invasions, forestalled European mediation and recognition of the Confederacy, perhaps prevented a Democratic victory in the northern elections of 1862 that might have inhibited the government's ability to carry on the war, and set the stage for the Emancipation Proclamation which enlarged the scope and purpose of the conflict."

Conclusion

If it was all about body count, then the South won at Perryville. However, attaining a strategic victory is rarely about body count.

After the Vietnam War, a U.S. and a North Vietnamese officer were discussing the conflict. The U.S. officer said, "We won nearly every battle." The North Vietnamese officer replied, "That is true, but it is also irrelevant."

There were no acts of strategic brilliance at Perryville. Both Buell and Bragg failed to take advantage of opportunities. More importantly, they both neglected to employ one of the most important soft skills an effective leader must possess. Neither man saw himself, his organization, or the enemy with the clarity necessary to be effective.

It was only by happenstance that the remaining Union corps finally assumed a position of advantage to threaten the Confederates at the end of the battle. It clearly was not the result of Buell's ingenuity.

Buell thought Bragg had 45,000 soldiers instead of the 16,500 that were actually available. If he had properly assessed Bragg's inferior numbers, instead of overestimating them, he could have brought the entire might of his 55,000 men to bear on the Rebels. Those 3-to-1 odds in Buell's favor would have most assuredly resulted in the total destruction of Bragg's army. Nonetheless, the Union commander ended up putting only 22,000 men into the fray.

Furthermore, Buell's overconfidence and rigidity further contributed to his failure to maneuver the corps effectively. He was convinced that the battle would begin on October 9. His arrogance clouded his judgment. He dismissed reports that the battle had begun and never went forward to see for himself. The *acoustic shadow* was as much present in Buell's character as it was an aspect of the terrain and wind direction.

Bragg, on the other hand, believed his army had numerical parity with Union forces. He was determined that the battle should begin immediately on the morning of October 8. The Rebel commander did not allow a thorough reconnaissance. Therefore, he thought he was assaulting Buell's weakness when, if fact, he directed his troops at the Federals' strength. Bragg trusted the *optical illusion* he saw because it represented a truth he wanted to see, not reality.

Brigadier General Sheridan started the battle prematurely for the Union in the early morning hours of October 8 during his search for a water source. The engagement was brought on by the cavalry commander's lack of situational awareness; nonetheless, he gained valuable ground in the engagement. However, Major General Gilbert gave up the key terrain because it was not a "part of the plan." Both he and Buell were not *adaptable* and failed to effectively react to the fog and friction of war.

Gilbert was a victim of an extreme example of the Peter Principle. He was promoted well beyond his level of incompetence, not having the experience to lead a regiment much less a corps. He was Buell's sycophant patsy. He should have diplomatically and respectfully explained the situation to his boss. Instead, he failed to exhibit an important aspect of good *followership*, that a subordinate must sometimes tell his superior information he may not want to hear.

As Donelson's brigade was being decimated by Union artillery on the Open Knob, Major General Cheatham showed *flexibility* by directing Brigadier General Maney to take out the cannons on the hill. Maney responded by *actively listening* to his junior officer when faced with an obstacle and pressed the fight. The Confederate commander *led by example* and *inspired* his troops in the attack.

Maney's assault was made less difficult because of the Union commander's poor leadership on the Open Knob and because soldiers were not properly cared for and trained. Brigadier General Terrill, another example of a person in charge promoted beyond his abilities, failed to *manage stress* and exhibit *emotional response control*. He got tunnel vision, and reverted to his comfort zone. He focused on his cannons rather than the employment of his brigade. As a result, his soldiers fell into a panicked and chaotic retreat.

Maney seized the hill. He took control of the Federal artillery because he *thought outside the box* and called indirect fire on the horses that moved the equipment. Brigadier General Maney postured the Confederates for a strategic victory if he could roll up the Union flank. However, he now faced an officer with similar soft skill prowess: Brigadier General John Starkweather.

Seeing the Confederates massing for an assault on his position, Starkweather *weighed risk* and made the difficult call to direct fire at both the Rebels and his own troops, stalling Maney's attack. Recognizing the situation was untenable, the Union commander ordered a withdrawal. When Starkweather's color sergeant was killed, Sergeant John Durham demonstrated *initiative*, picked up the flag, and led a counterattack that allowed Starkweather's brigade to assume a defensible position.

With his brigade safely behind a stonewall on a steep hill, Starkweather repelled the Rebel assault and saved the Union flank. In spite of the Army of the Ohio commander's failures, Colonel John Starkweather turned what was initially a tactical defeat into a strategic victory.

It would be bold to assert that soft skills alone won the day at the Battle of Perryville. The Union generally had better equipment, more rifled muskets and cannons, and a slight numerical advantage. They possessed good terrain, along with the benefit of the railed fence and other obstacles, which made a Confederate attack more difficult. The Federals also had the benefit of purpose provided by President Lincoln in his message that Kentucky had to be saved for the Union to prevail. Jefferson Davis's instructions to Bragg, on the other hand, were to help ensure the inauguration of a governor sympathetic to the South. Needless to say, the purpose Lincoln provided was much more clear and decisive.

The majority of leaders in both armies possessed good hard skills. Most had attended West Point and had previous combat experience. However, it is interesting that the two most effective leaders in the battle, Maney and Starkweather, graduated from schools other than the U.S. Military Academy. Maney went to the Nashville Seminary and Starkweather attended Union College. Maybe a liberal arts education played a role in developing their soft skills, but it's hard to tell.

Soft skills may not have been the sole contributor to battlefield success at Perryville, but they were the deciding factor. Furthermore, the failure of leaders to exhibit soft skills nearly cost both sides any chance of winning. The leaders that mastered those intangible qualities such as initiative, adaptability, empathy, creativity, and thinking outside the box, among all the others, made the difference on the battlefield.

We should all strive to become experts in the soft skills and become the best leader possible. I understood that throughout most of my career. I was fortunate to have superb men and women who modeled the soft skills that separated good leaders from great ones. However, it was an experience I had not long before deploying to Iraq for the second time that entrenched the purpose of good leadership into my soul.

When I was a basic training battalion commander, I always went out on the parade field after graduations to see the new soldiers and meet their parents and loved ones. After a particular ceremony, I approached a mom and dad with their son. He stood tall in his dress uniform and black beret. I congratulated the soldier and said to the mom and dad that they must be proud of their boy. The mother thanked me and said, "I'm proud of all my boys. His oldest brother is in Afghanistan. He's been there about four months." She then paused. Her hands then went to her lips and chin as if to prevent the words she was about to say from coming out of her mouth. She faltered, seeming to lose her balance for a moment. Her husband put his hand on her shoulder to steady her. The woman then stood straight and tall like her son and said, "We lost our middle son in Iraq two months ago before this one came here for basic training. I'm sure he's watching down on us though. I am so very proud of him. He died saving one of his buddies. They gave him a Bronze Star for Valor."

My stomach dropped to my knees. I could not believe what I just heard and said the only thing that came to my mind, telling her that I was so sorry for her loss. This woman stood even more erect. It was like she grew larger before my eyes and assumed the posture of a giant towering over us. She then said in a resolute, almost stern voice, "Don't be sorry, Colonel. The nation will now have all my children. It is the least I can do."

I came away from that experience with an understanding, more than ever, of the tremendous responsibility we have as leaders. Mothers, fathers, spouses, and siblings put their trust in us to care for the people they love most.

Whether in business or the military we have to hone both our hard and soft skills. We must burn the midnight oil to become experts in the technical skills of our craft and sharpen those abilities that require the emotional intelligence to connect us with our people. It is the men and women who put themselves on the line every day to accomplish the mission that matter most. It's them, not us, that ensure our success. Our duty is to be the very best leaders possible for those who count on us.

It is the least we can do.

ABOUT THE AUTHOR

Colonel Fred Johnson (USA, Retired) served in the Army for 29 years and he is the author of the book *Five Wars: A Soldier's Journey to Peace*. Fred has told the story of his journey through five wars on the stage during the Moth GrandSlam, with the Louisville StoryTellers, on the Moth Radio Hour Podcast and in *Reader's Digest*. Fred was commissioned as a 2nd Lieutenant of Infantry through the Reserve Officer Training Corps at Wofford College in Spartanburg, S.C. in 1985 where he earned Bachelor of Arts degrees in Government and Sociology.

He first went to war in 1991 during OPERATION DESERT STORM and participated in the liberation of Kuwait. In 1996, he participated in OPERATION JOINT ENDEAVOR in Bosnia, which helped end Serbian genocide of Bosnian Muslims. In 2006-2007 during OPERATION IRAQI FREEDOM, and at the height of the Surge, Fred received the Bronze Star for Valor during OPERATION ARROWHEAD RIPPER and the liberation of Baqubah from Al Qaeda. In his last combat deployment as a part of OPERATION ENDURING FREEDOM, Fred was the advisor to the most senior military officer in the Afghan National Army. In addition to the Bronze Star for Valor, Fred was awarded the Legion of Merit with Oak Leaf Cluster, the Bronze Star for Service with two Oak Leaf Clusters and the Meritorious Service Medal with four Oak Leaf

Clusters. He is a graduate of the U.S. Army Ranger, Airborne and Air Assault schools, the Command and General Staff College and the U.S. Army War College.

Since retiring from the Army in 2014, Fred has continued his service, now in Louisville, Kentucky, as a veteran and social justice advocate and has worked as a fundraiser for two non-profits. Fred founded the Perryville Battlefield Leadership Experience, an immersive training seminar that teaches executive leader lessons learned through the lens of Civil War leaders who fought at Perryville in 1862. He is the co-founder of Shakespeare with Veterans, a program dedicated to help veterans deal with the challenges transitioning from military service and help them overcome combat trauma and PTSD. He also serves as a volunteer with Restorative Justice Louisville. Fred is from Centralia, Illinois, and along with his B.A. degrees he has two Masters Degrees. He is married to Dr. Laura Johnson and they have a daughter Madelyn.

To learn more about the Perryville Battlefield Leadership Experience, schedule an event or have Colonel Johnson speak for your group, Fred can be contacted at:

fredwjohnsonjr74@gmail.com or by phone at 803-741-4540. Also visit his website at fivewars.com to learn more bout his book *Five Wars: A Soldier's Journey to Peace*.

www.ingramcontent.com/pod-product-compliance
Lightning Source LLC
La Vergne TN
LVHW021459080426
835509LV00018B/2339